Miracles Appear When
Loved Ones Are Near

Ciara O' Malley

Published by Book Hub Publishing with Offices in Galway and Limerick.

Partnered with Rare Swan Press, Zug, Switzerland.

First Edition 2020 ISBN: 978-1-8381691-9-0

DEDICATION

This book is dedicated to my beloved David. Thank you for never leaving my side.

ACKNOWLEDGMENTS

I would like to thank my parents, Mary and Patrick, my sister Lindsey and my brother Ryan. Thank you for always being there and supporting me in everything I do. I love you all unconditionally.

I would like to thank David's parents, Angela and Michael, and sister Aoife. I am forever grateful for the love and support you have shown to me. One blessing from this journey is the unbreakable bond we now all have. I will forever be your piece of David and you will be mine.

To all my friends, family and everyone who supported me on this journey. I am so blessed and grateful to have you all in my life. From the bottom of my heart, I love each and every one of you. I wouldn't be where I am today without you all.

I would like to thank my Publishing House and, in particular, my editors Susan McKenna, Niall MacGiolla Bhuí and Anna Gray. Thank you for being a constant stream of support. It has been a pleasure to work with each and every one of you.

I would also like to thank the incredibly talented, Avril Egan, who illustrated the cover for the book. It could not be any more perfect.

To everyone who played a part in supporting us to find David and bring him home, my heart exuberates gratitude to each and every one of you. The kindness, love and generosity shown to us was something out of this world, so from the bottom of my heart - thank you.

Thank you everyone who donated to the David Gavin search fund. Through these donations we were able to get the resources and services needed to make the search for David successful.

To everyone who prayed, lit candles, and sent us blessings to help find David, thank you. Keep praying, keep wishing never give up hope or stop believing in miracles.

Miracles Appear When Loved Ones Are Near

What is a divinely guided plan? That is not something I would have asked a few years ago. It was not on my agenda, so I did not need to know. Now I am adamant my life has just turned into one divinely guided plan. Only when I think I have 'sussed' things out just even a little bit, something else is thrown into the woodwork.

I would not have called myself a spiritual person before my life took a very different direction. Fortunately for me, I realised spirituality and knowing are part of something so much bigger, bigger than I can comprehend, and it significantly changed my life. It has led me to question everything, my beliefs, my values. It has given me an understanding that we are supported even within the depths of turmoil.

So, what is a divinely guided plan? As I see it, a divinely guided plan means that a force higher than us is helping us out, or has a plan for us. Have you ever felt like something was supposed to happen? There is no real logic, just a knowing. Well, that is the way I feel about this book and my life in general. I knew before I even finished writing this book, there was a plan for it. There was no logic to it, and I could not explain it, but I knew I had to write it. I knew that it had a purpose. My intuition knew nothing else other than the fact that I was destined to write it. I believe that I was gifted a journey – that my life experience and the wisdom I gained from trying to put the pieces of my life back together could help others. If you are reading this, there may be a plan behind it also. I fully believe nothing ever

1

happens by chance. Ironically enough, a few years ago David and I were on holidays in New Jersey, and he bought me a bracelet that had the following written on it 'everything happens for a reason'. Even then, I think he was guiding me on a journey I had no idea I was to embark on.

I hope you get comfort from this book and that it helps open your eyes to the enchanting world we live in. As I said before, 'nothing happens by chance' and I think we only refer to this saying in relation to the good things that happen in life. Still, unfortunately, it also refers to all the challenges we are dealt with too, as I was to discover later.

I am so grateful for all life has offered me in my 30 years here. If you asked me three years ago what turning 30 might look like, I would have told you I had it all figured out. I would have been engaged to my teen sweetheart David, and we would have been starting a new chapter in our lives. This chapter would have involved settling down and even commencing to think about marriage and starting a family. The funny thing about life is that it does not go by our plans.

Life decided to throw a serious and unwelcome curveball at me. You could even say life came tumbling in on top of me. This ball game was one that was certainly not in my plan, and one I never thought in a million years could ever happen to me.

Whilst in Canada, my beloved David was involved in a tragic drowning accident, and just like that, he was gone. Life as I knew it, was over. Everything familiar to me had changed, and there was nothing I could do to stop it.

To make things even more complicated, David's body was missing. So, as well as trying to get my head around the fact he was gone, I was also trying to understand that we did not know where he was.

With all the power and might we had, and I say 'we', because there were so many involved in this journey, we persevered through all the pain. Against all the odds, ten months later, we found David's body and brought him home to Ireland to lay him to rest.

I was so grateful because, for a long time, even the chance of finding him looked like being out of our reach. But for me, that was when a whole other journey began. I had a choice to stay stuck in the depths of despair, or try and navigate my way through this loss and grief. It was either stay stuck or find out who Ciara was without my beloved David by my side. David was all I knew and wanted; we had been together for ten years as a couple. It petrified me to contemplate life without him, but I chose to give it a try.

After years of resisting any change and wearing my pain and suffering as a courtship, I tightly clung on to my grief; it was all I had left of David. It felt safe at the time; it felt like the closest thing I had to him; every tear I shed was a tear of love. But it got to a point where the grief was consuming me. I had become all grief and no Ciara.

This book will discuss some of the challenges I went through on this journey, and even though David was well and truly gone, love remained. Through this love, he showed me a magical and magnificent side of life that I feel compelled to share with you all.

For a long time, I could not fathom why I had been dealt these cards. I did not think I was a bad person, so why had something so awful happened to me? I know bad things happen every day of the week, but for so long I was utterly consumed by what had occurred in my life. At times, I wondered would I ever start to feel half right again.

Throughout the darkness of this journey, which I can assure you at times were bleak, I started to see glimmers of light. I began to see that even though my heart was utterly broken, somehow there was a bigger plan to all of this. I started to slowly understand that, somehow, for some crazy reason, this was always destined to be my life. I had to go through something so soul-destroying to find who I was and the reason I was sent here.

I can, hand on my heart, say that this journey to finding my inner strength to heal myself is my second proudest moment to date. The first being, finding David and bringing him home.

To even think I am writing this book feels so surreal. After everything I have been through over the last few years, I would have been happy for a quiet life. But this book felt like a scratch itching to get out. It is so hard to explain, but I know that this book is destined to help others, to give them light and hope and help navigate whatever challenges life throws at them. In finding my way to the light, I have been exposed to a whole new level of self-awareness. I believe everything we need to heal ourselves is inside of each and every one of us.

And what was even more magical and beautiful was the fact I found a connection to my loved one David in spirit. Our loved ones may leave us in the physical sense, but their love is always with us, and when they leave this world, I believe their primary duty is to protect and mind us. They are good at that. Even in our loneliest of moments, they are there right beside us, holding us, wishing we, too, could feel their presence.

If my English teacher ever reads this book, I am sure he would agree that, out of the class, I was most definitely the least likely to write a book. This book is not an academic piece of work, it is written from my heart and soul, hoping that my experience can help others embark on their own journeys. I could have written a book on the trauma of what we went through at the lake and the nightmare that was my new life, a nightmare that did not go away but merely replayed and replayed. I had no option but to face the reality that this was my new life, whether I liked it or not.

It is not my belief to tell other people what to do or tell other people that they should follow what I did on my journey. Instead, I want my story to inspire you to find a truth and healing path that best suits you and your needs.

The purpose of this book is to show people that we can rise from our darkest moments, that there is light at the end of the tunnel and I am proof of that. But most importantly, it is to remind us all that our loved ones are always with us. I am excited for you all to see how David never left my side. He just had to show me he was around and I had to be willing to accept and be receptive to all the signs.

The Beautiful Soul That is David

David touched so many people's lives in his short lifetime here. I am so eternally blessed to have such a unique soul in my life. I say soul because he is still with me. He never left. Souls cannot leave us; when we get an understanding of that, we start to view the world as a different place, one where we are still connected by love. Love never dies.

He is a kind, gentle soul with an energetic passion for life. His warm smile is so inviting. A smile that lights up his entire face. A smile that would make you want to talk to him. In the physical world, he was the kindest person; he would do anything to help you if he could at all. He loved his family and friends. He loved having fun and spending time with the people who mattered most to him. His eyes would light up a room. He had a great perspective on life and just wanted to make the most of it. Now, on the pitch, it was a bit different, David took no prisoners, and his true passion was his love of Gaelic football. I would often joke that I was his second girlfriend. I loved seeing him so in love and passionate about something.

7

Playing football lit a fire in David, it sparked so many excellent qualities in him, and he was known on and off the field as an all-round gentleman. He adored it, and he was so talented at it, yet he was the humblest person you could ever meet. He had an impressive football CV, and his determination and drive was always pushing him on to succeed more in all aspects of his life. He was continually seeking out adventure and was always looking for the next one to embark on. If adrenaline was involved, David was there with bells on. A few years previously, he was introduced to skiing which became another love in his life. This made moving to Canada even more appealing as it meant easy access to the ski slopes. He was highly intelligent and always willing and eager to learn new things. David excelled in his career choice and was still trying to upskill himself at the time of his accident.

David was, and always will be, the love of my life. At such a young age, he taught me how to love in the purest form. A love that was magnetic and bonded two people together. A love I never knew until I met him, but it just felt so special and right. I knew I was so lucky to experience it at such a young age. We were not perfect, but I would not have changed anything about us for the world. David taught me to love unconditionally with all my heart. A love where our two souls felt safe and secure with a deep knowing that in his lifetime here, we were destined to spend our lives together. Even though his time was cut short, this love remained and took on a different form. His love pushed me on to be strong and resilient in the presence of adversity and deep pain.

Where it all Began

I was 17 years old when I first met David. It was New Year's Eve, and we were both at a Saw Doctors concert in our local town. It would have been hard to miss him as he stretched over 6 foot tall.

The concert was finishing up when we struck up a conversation; I could tell he was lovely; he was also easy on the eye which was an added plus. I wanted to talk to him, but I was preoccupied as I had lost my jacket. David being ever the gentleman, agreed to help me find it. We searched up and down looking for it, and you can imagine my delight at finding it. I was even more delighted when it meant I could talk to him properly. After that night that was it, two hearts bonded forever more.

My fondest memory of my youth would be rushing home from school to log onto MSN messenger to talk to David. I knew quickly he was someone special, someone I wanted to keep in my life. We were relatively young, but we knew that we were going to spend the rest of our lives together.

Life was good, but we both had a yearning for more. We decided to embark on a journey of a lifetime and see what the world had to offer us. We decided to move to Canada. And that was where life took on a different path for both David and I.

The Big Move to Canada

For so long, we spoke about moving to Canada, in September 2016, David said "Right, let's go". At the time, I didn't bat an eyelid as we had been on about it for so long, I just thought this time was the same. However, something was different; he started looking into it; and I knew this time we were going to go.

We were so excited that we were finally doing it; we were biting the bullet and moving. It all just felt so right, and everything was working out perfectly.

Before we left Ireland, I suggested we have a small going away party; it was a big deal as we were moving across the other side of the world. David was not into any kind of fuss but, equally, he would not turn down an excuse for a party as he loved socialising. Eventually, I twisted his arm and he agreed. We had a great night with memories and pictures we can now always cherish. Reflecting, it was like the universe decided we would have one big celebration before leaving. David left Ireland with a bang; little did we know at that time his fate was already sealed.

The Canadian Lifestyle

We arrived in Vancouver, a place we would later call our home and it could not have been any more perfect. We didn't know anyone, but that did not matter because we had each other. We both always had a fond love of the sea and spoke about one day living near it. You can imagine our delight when we found a lovely little apartment beside the beach.

After a few weeks in Vancouver, exploring and enjoying the local surroundings, we made the decision that it was time to start looking for jobs. We both would have been happy not working for another while, but unfortunately, the bank accounts were telling us otherwise!

Getting jobs turned out to be a lot easier than we thought and luck was on our side as we managed to find employment in our desired fields of work. David got offered multiple jobs in the line of data analytics. All his Christmases came at once when he was able to take his pick of jobs. I got a job as a Manager within a social care setting. We were both delighted to get positions that were Monday to Friday 9-5. This meant we could spend the evenings and weekends together. It was like the stars were aligning for us in Canada.

Vancouver was cool, vibrant, and full of culture; there were also so many places to eat. David and I always had a fond love of food. Often, when we would finish work, we would meet each other at the beach. We would sit on the sand often accompanied by food, the sun glaring down on us with not a care in the world.

The Canadian lifestyle suited us, and we were relishing in it.

We also had the chance to indulge in skiing, which had become David's favourite hobby. To say he fell in love with skiing was an understatement. He could not have been any more excited to be living so close to the slopes.

I liked skiing, but I was nowhere near as good as him. Keeping up to him often involved a lot of screeching and landing on a colour slope that petrified me.

David had started playing Gaelic football whilst in Vancouver, and somehow, he had even managed to get me to join a team. This was a big deal as I would not have considered myself the sporty type. He was proud as punch; I was going for fun, but I think he had notions of trying to make a professional out of me! He had the patience of a saint, and he even gave me a few lessons before I went to my first training session. First on his list was to teach me how to solo. It gave me a laugh, and I played along and pretended to be as serious about it as he was.

To make life even more perfect, we had also made some fantastic friends, who turned out to be more like our own little Canadian family. With our weekends free, we would take full advantage and make sure they were action-packed and crammed to the gills with activities. We would often hire a car and head off with our friends skiing. It was ideal as the nearest slopes were only half an hour drive away. We had the best of both worlds, living beside the beach and yet also so close to the slopes. You could go skiing in the morning and then come back and relax by the beach.

Vancouver was so majestic and we wanted to see as many of the sights as possible. We would often get up early on a Saturday to go hiking, cycling or do something activity-based. We had the right balance, and after our activities we would have a few 'sociables' in one of the local pubs with our Canadian family, often staying until late in the morning, enjoying ourselves with our new friends. Life really was at its peak, and we made sure we made the most of every second of it. There was no hanging around, we were always busy, looking for our next adventure. It was so exciting, and we felt so lucky to have met like-minded people with which to share these experiences.

A Blissful Weekend

On one of the weekends before David's accident, we spent the most blissful weekend with our friends. We hired a car and headed up to the ski slopes. That morning, David woke up and had a smile beaming from cheek to cheek. We picked up our friends and spent a few hours up on the slopes. David was showing us his new skills, and had recently discovered how to do a full 360 jump, making us all watch on as he showed off his latest talent! He had little fear and could try his hand to anything.

When we finished on the slopes, we took full advantage of having the car and decided to go for a drive. We had no plan, no destination but that made it even more enjoyable. We pulled into a bay and got out of the car and had a look around.

We sat in awe, looking out into the bay as one of us spotted a whale. We sat there for a while, our eyes following the whale's movement. No one there but us six new friends who were exploring the beautiful and captivating nature sites Canada had to offer. They did not know back then, but these friends turned out to be the glue that held me together early on in this journey.

Getting the News

On June 30th 2017, after living our Canadian dream for five blissful months, my life crumbled before my very eyes. 'Crumbled' sounds as if it fell apart in pieces, but it was more like a boulder that came and knocked the life, as I knew it, from under my feet. I mentioned earlier that up to this, life was amazing and could not have been going any better. Even writing this, I am wondering would it have been easier if we did not like Canada or if things had not run as smoothly? This used to haunt me but now looking back, I am so grateful to have had this fantastic time, and I really treasure it. I often wonder if David somehow knew his time was coming to an end because we crammed so much into the months while living in Vancouver.

It was my birthday. I had just turned 27. That morning, I left our apartment and headed to work as I usually did. David had left the day before to go to a football tournament in Calgary. As I headed off on the bus to work it was like any other day, the only difference being it was my birthday, it was a Friday and a long weekend stretched out ahead. We had big plans to celebrate; a group of us were going to the beach for a BBQ. I left work feeling proud as punch I had gotten through the week and made it to the other side. I had heard from David earlier that morning and told him I would ring him after work.

On the bus home, I phoned David, but it went straight to voice mail. I expected that he would call me back as soon as he could. Sitting on the bus, I stared out at the beautiful day. I felt so lucky to be exactly where I was at that moment in time. Do you ever see those people on the bus that just look 'blissfully joyful' - well, on that day it was me. I had a smile beaming from cheek to cheek sitting on the bus, in utter awe of my current life.

I stopped at the shop on the way home to buy some groceries to bring to the BBQ. My biggest dilemma in that moment was, 'what was I going to buy?' I pottered around the shop, picked up the goods and walked back to our apartment. The weather was warm, and I began to work up a sweat walking back to our apartment. I remember thinking I would have to wear something cool; otherwise, I was going to roast on the beach.

I went back to our apartment and put on some music and started to get ready. I called David again, but there was still no reply. Generally, by now, I would have been worried, but for some reason I wasn't. Unknown to me at this time, his accident had already occurred. I still just assumed he would call me back as soon as he could.

I remember hearing that some people get a 6th sense that something bad had happened, that certainly was not the case for me. If anything, I felt freer and happier than ever. I often wonder did David send me this elevated feeling of joy because I remember going from a place of ultimate joy to crash, burn, despair where I remained for a long time.

Weeks previously to this, I begged David not to go to the tournament and stay in Vancouver with me for my birthday. We always used to joke that I was his second love after football; he was stone mad about it.

After ten years of being with him, football was as much a part of my life as it was his. As it stood, he was going to the tournament rain, hail or shine.

Instead, we celebrated my birthday the night before he left. We met each other after work and strolled around Vancouver in the sun; we had a lovely meal together, which of course had to end in ice cream. It was so perfect.

I was still dancing around my apartment while at the same time sticking my head out the window for air, as our apartment did not have air conditioning. I was doing my makeup when I received a phone call from one of my friends saying they were on their way over.

I asked who was coming and she replied all four of them were on their way. David and I had made lots of friends in Vancouver, but we hung out with two sets of couples most of the time. I remember thinking how great it was that they were on their way as normally they were late. This probably should have been another red flag I ought to have noticed. Still, I was just so delighted they were coming over, and I was excited for all the fun we were going to have.

At this stage, I tried to call David again still with no reply. I got a little bit frustrated and left him a voice message asking him to contact me straight away. It was not enough to stress me out and I still assumed he would call me back. I thought maybe he had lost his phone or had no coverage and that he might borrow one of his friend's phones to ring me when he could. Writing this, I wonder why this did not alarm me earlier that something was wrong. It was like for a few short hours

I was protected from the reality of what was about to happen for just a little while longer.

It was also so unlike me, as normally, my anxiety would have peaked by now. David used to joke and call me a worrier. It was true. The smallest of things would have me fretting.

The doorbell rang, and I buzzed them in. I cheerily opened the door to greet the four best friends David and I had made in Vancouver. If I wasn't so consumed in my own little bubble, the look on their faces probably would have hit home with me, but no, I was still in my world, feeling happy and free. On another day, maybe I would have been able to read the signs but not that day. I think I told them how excited I was, which I am sure made what they were about to say to me much harder.

They all walked into our little apartment and asked me to sit on the couch. I felt spoilt, and I thought they were about to give me my birthday present. I sat down on the couch as requested with a look of anticipation on my face.

I remember feeling so special how lucky was I to have made such amazing friends who wanted to celebrate my birthday with me. And then, just like that, my bubble burst, the air completely deflated for me. To this day, I cannot remember who said what, or how the words came out, but all I remember hearing were the words 'David' repeatedly. Nothing would ever have prepared me for what was going to come next.

My head heard "David, lake, trouble". I remember looking at my friends, their faces said it all. They were completely and utterly shocked, and I knew by their reaction, this was terrible news. Really bad. My cheer went straight to fear. I think I sat on the couch in complete shock, as if someone had just switched the lights off.

Instantly, I remembered I had not been able to reach him all day and my heart just fell into pieces. I counted in my head and realised he hadn't answered the phone on numerous occasions throughout the day. I looked at my four friends standing there in our little apartment holding back the tears, trying to be strong for me. This was very real, and at that moment my life changed forever.

My first reaction was to pace up and down the kitchen and then go into the bathroom and take a breath. Whatever was going on right now was coming at a thundering pace. All I wanted was to go somewhere and hide. I remember sitting on the toilet seat, and my first reaction was to call David's phone. It went straight to his voicemail as it did previously. I wanted to cry, to scream, to break something but I just froze. In my head, I prayed to God or whoever was up there 'please let this not be real'. I quickly realised sitting in the bathroom was not doing anything for this situation. So, I went back out into the kitchen and got as much information as I could.

I remember asking lots of questions; little did I know they did not know much more than I did. My friends informed me they had been told a few hours previous, but they wanted to come and tell me in person before I heard from anyone else. I knew I had to speak to someone who was there at the lake with David. I got a phone number and made the call to one of David's friends who was at the lake. I am sure I sounded erratic on the phone, but I needed to know exactly what was going on. I remember hoping and praying they would tell me that they had got it wrong, and he was ok or at least give me some glimmer of hope.

They told me they were currently at Kinbasket Lake and that the Royal Canadian Mounted Police were there searching for David. They told me he had jumped off the bridge and had not resurfaced. I remember sounding frantic, "What do you mean, not resurfaced?" I knew what resurfaced meant; my soul just longed to hear something else. All they could do was answer my question, David had come up for a breath, waved up to his friends who were on the bridge where he jumped in and then was pulled back under the water. Listening to that news, my body experienced emotions I had never felt before. I started to feel like something had taken it over, and it all just felt so weird. I wanted a hug; someone to hold me and tell me everything was going to be ok. But not just anybody, I needed my David. He always managed to make things better.

It was getting apparent very quickly that even though I had people around me, I was very much alone. David was the only person who I really listened to or could calm me down. You know the way they say 'your other half?' Well, David really was the other half of me. How was I going to figure this out alone?

I got off the phone, and my head was spinning. I could see vividly what had happened to David and all I wanted was the image in my mind to go away, the awful picture of David being pulled under and then gone. My heart could not cope with that realisation. Hence, with every fibre of my imagination, I pretended everything was somehow going to be ok. It must have been a psychological response because I was not willing to deal with the nightmare I had been thrown into.

'David would not leave me; he knows I would not be able to cope without him. We had our whole life planned together; this is just a little blip; everything was going to be ok somehow'. Deep down, I knew this was never the case, but I needed something to push me along because I knew I had to get to the lake and brave the elements and tackle this head-on.

Getting to the Lake and Facing this Head-on

During everything, my friends were just terrific and took control of the situation. I often reflect on how hard it must have been for them. They were so brave, kind and strong and I know David chose them to be part of this journey. Nothing is by chance, and the role they played was divinely guided too. I knew I had to get to the lake as soon as possible. I had two options to get there, to fly or drive and I decided it was quicker to drive there. Without even thinking about it, my friends offered to drive me as they had a car. It was a 5-hour journey, so we needed to get on the road as soon as possible.

I was informed by the local police that they wanted me to wait in my apartment so they could formally tell me what had happened. The frustration kicked in when I waited over an hour and they still had not arrived. I did not have time to wait around for them. I needed to immediately leave and get to the lake as soon as possible.

Before we left, I knew I had to make a phone call; one which would equally turn other people's lives upside down and into chaos. I rang my parents and asked them to deliver the news to David's family. It was late when I rang my parents and getting a phone call that late startled them. I found it hard to get the words out; it was the first time I had to verbally tell anyone what had happened. They knew by my reaction on the phone that something terrible had happened. I somehow managed to get the words out in a way they understood.

I could hear in my parents voices they were heartbroken, and they too were under no illusions at how bad this may be. During that phone call, my heart shattered, and the reality of what was going on was starting to sink in. My head kept imagining David's parents and sister getting the news feeling helpless on the other side of the world. At least I could quickly get to the lake and figure out what was going on.

Being ever the optimist, I was under the illusion we were going to find David safe and well. I was going to grill him for putting us all through this nightmare, and he was going to promise never to do it again, and that would be it. One of the stories I had created in my head was that David had swam off fast, as he would have been a strong swimmer and he was currently making his way back to the shore.

At this stage, my phone did not stop making noise; everyone had heard of what was going on. I know it was kind, people sending messages saying they were thinking of me, but in each message I received, I remember thinking 'this is real'. I just wanted to press a pause button on my life because I didn't know how to cope with what was going on.

The journey to the lake involved me having numerous phone calls with the police service and one with David's family, which was just utterly soul-destroying. We all tried to remain positive and only hope for the best. I remember somehow falling asleep in the car on the journey, probably not even for a few minutes. The first few moments waking up, I remember my mind being silent, and then I remembered what was going on. For those few short minutes, the nightmare was gone, and my mind was blank. The dread that came on awakening scared me so much; it frightened me as did the thought of having to go to sleep again.

The car journey was mostly silent - what could anyone say about what was going on? We were supposed to be on the beach celebrating, but instead, we were all in a car not prepared for what was coming next. The silence was chilling and you could feel the energy between us all. We were petrified of what was going to greet us when we arrived at the lake. We knew we were getting close and you could feel the mood in the car just sink. I had spoken to one of David's friends, and they knew we were due to arrive very soon.

As we approached the dirt road down to the lake, I thought my insides were going to pop out. The road alone was enough to have stopped me from going down there never mind anything else. It did not help that it was 5am in the morning. It was dark, dull and miserable, which mirrored the way we all felt.

An anger came over me as I questioned, 'Why would you want to drive down that road?' It was full of bends and potholes. A road you would try best to avoid in normal circumstances. Arriving at the lake, I could see the bridge in the distance, this was all getting very real. Looking at the bridge, I knew this was a lot worse than my protective mind was letting me believe. Still, in that moment, I chose for another while longer to replay the scenario in my mind that we would find David alive and all would be well. I stared at the bridge in shock knowing that was the last place he stood. In that moment I prayed. I prayed somehow everything would be ok. I prayed because I did not know what else to do.

I did not think I was a spiritual person before all this. I would have always been open-minded into exploring ideas outside of the social norm. David would often have referred to me as a fairy. I knew I believed in something, but I was not sure what that was. One thing I knew for sure was that whenever something bad happened, I always prayed. This time it was the most horrendous thing that had happened and I needed something, anything to help give me strength and courage.

Trying to Find Hope and Begging for Help

I prayed like my life depended on it, which it did. I asked David for a sign and stared out onto the lake, hoping to see something. I saw a glimmer of a little golden fish. On such a dark, dull, misty morning, the sparkling of that golden fish brought me a glimmer of light. It sparked something in me. I knew someone had sent me that fish to give me some hope. That it did, hope that things might be ok, hope that there is someone looking out for me.

I had now been at the lake for over an hour; nothing was happening, and the frustration was kicking in. I remember feeling so helpless having to wait for another few hours for all the services to arrive and continue the search. David was missing, and nobody was doing anything! I was struggling to understand why David decided to come to this place at all. It felt eerie to me like it was the kind of place terrible things happen in all the time.

I wanted to do what I could to find David, but I did not know where to start. We began asking locals who were staying on the campsite to help us as we didn't know what to do. I remember asking a man to help us. The words came out of my mouth, and the shock just overwhelmed me. I had just asked a man to help us look for my boyfriend who was somewhere in the vast amount of water that I saw before me. I had never seen anything like this lake before. It looked like a monster, and only when we got out into the water did we understand what we were dealing with.

The man agreed, and a few of us went with him in his boat. As I sat on this random man's boat on that cold misty morning, I stared out into the water and a realisation set in, we were looking for David, my David who up until a few hours ago was very much alive. We were looking for him; he was gone.

The kind man told us he had a 'fish finder' on his boat. It was an electronic piece of equipment that scans the water to look for fish. He briefly showed us how it worked and we stared at that screen, looking for David.

It was so strange and obscure instead of looking for fish we were looking for David. It was only then I knew we were dealing with a more serious situation than I had ever imagined. I had never heard of a fish finder before, but there I was staring at the screen trying to find David. My scenario of him being alive was slipping away. I felt sick at what we were going through. It just didn't feel real. That man was so kind to bring us out on his boat but eventually, it got to a point where he had to bring us back in.

The Lake

There was nothing we could do except wait for the professional services to arrive. Every minute felt like an hour, but at the same time, it was apparent we needed time to be on our side. As the day started to brighten, people started arising from the campsite. Lots of people. As it was peak season, it was busy. The campsite's main attraction was the lake, so that was where everyone circulated.

Eventually, the search and rescue team landed and they did a sweep of the lake. On their return, they told us we would have to wait for a specialist dive team to come, and it could take a few days. It was incredibly frustrating to hear, but there was not much we could do but wait. The locals were excellent; they would take us out on their boats a few times a day to do a search.

The first night, I was terrified to close my eyes, but at the same time, my mind and body was shattered. An exceedingly kind, generous couple let me spend the night with them in their cabin so I would not have to sleep in a tent. As I lay in bed, I could hear the couple talk in the room below. I did not know this couple; I was too tired to thoroughly think about how peculiar this all was. The next morning, I awoke early and crept down to the lake to try and get a few minutes to myself. As I stared out at the lake, I felt so numb, yet it was all starting to feel so real. That day was like the previous day, there was little movement, and we all felt so hopeless as we baked in the blistering heat.

Over the next few days, my priority of finding David alive quickly turned to locating him. One day, someone said the exact words "David's situation was never a rescue; it was always a recovery". It was like they had just come up and stuck a big pin into my core and it burst right before my very eyes.

I knew this deep in my soul, but hearing the words just tore my heart in half. At this stage, David's family and some of my family had arrived at the lake. It quickly became apparent we were up against the odds, every day we learnt more about the conditions of the lake and finding him moved further from our reach.

I remember praying to David every day that today would be the day we found him. For the first few days, I longed to see him alive. Now I just pleaded with him to help us find his body. My mind struggled to come to terms with the fact; we were never going to see him alive, it suffocated me. But I still pushed through. We all did.

At this stage, the outpouring of support we got from around the world was genuinely immense, and a GoFundMe account was set up to help us find David. We were truly blown away by the kindness and support offered to us by people who were touched by our story. It really did give us the strength and courage to push on daily with our goal of finding him and bringing him home to Ireland.

Bringing People Together

David was always a people person; his kind caring nature made him someone you would want to spend time with. On the first few days at the lake, I felt he pulled people together by such tragic circumstances. We were all at the lakeside together. We all shared a common purpose to find David. We would spend the whole day out searching for him, and then in the evening, we would all gather around the campsite looking out onto the lake. It was soothing knowing that we were still so close to him.

Often, there would be a massive group of us, people who selflessly dedicated their time to help us find David. Some of these people we had never even met and this truly touched my heart. We were like a big molded family. There was David's family, some of my family, our friends, volunteers, some of the local GAA team members and, most importantly, all the professionals from the services helping us search for him.

I believe David handpicked each person who was there and every role was equally important.

Merging with my New Reality

The campsite was small and we quickly became part of the furniture often feeling like we had been there for years rather than a few days. Anxieties were high and our only priority was finding David. Nothing else mattered.

I would often watch families on their holidays spend time doing water activities such as fishing. It was a bit of a kick in the teeth to see people so happy and having fun with not a care in the world. I often wondered; would my life ever go back to simpler times.

One day when the search boat was getting ready to launch into the water, it was so apparent to see the two different worlds. The search team had sectioned off some of the lake and were getting ready to start, yet a few metres away was a lady in a bikini on a sunchair. We were all in the same campsite, but at that moment our lives could not have been any more different.

I would have done anything to be sitting on that chair, where my only concern was whether I was going to get sunburned or not. In that moment I was frustrated, and in my head, I said a few harsh words. The reality was that her life was not affected by this. That day, she was doing exactly what she was supposed to be doing, enjoying her holiday. Grief can send you a little bit crazy. Scrap that. I mean crazy. In my eyes, I could not understand how that lady could not see what was going on. My mind was entirely on high alert; I just wanted to find David.

Leaving No Stone Unturned

I was going to make sure no stone was left unturned if it meant we found David. Every day, there were boats out searching and we were doing everything we possibly could. We had highly qualified professionals helping us with the search. It was so reassuring as they had a lot of experience and were confident that they could help us.

It was so frustrating that we were doing everything we possibly could to find David however, we were not reaping the rewards. We were highly active in the search and that helped pull us along. Every day we would go out on boats searching, scanning the water hoping David had resurfaced. We had been informed this could be a possibility, and we had to cover all avenues.

We became familiar with the electrical equipment called sonar that scanned the water looking for David's body. This equipment would be placed into the water and we would then watch the screen on the top of the boat, looking for something that could resemble his body. It is hard to explain, but we knew exactly what his body would look like on that screen. The only problem was we were not getting anything that resembled this.

Glimmers of Hope

In the first few weeks, we had a few moments where we thought we had found David. One day we had the canine search team out on the water searching. These dogs are exceptionally well trained, and they work off the scent the deceased body releases. We all watched on frantically as the dog howled at a particular spot not too far from where David had jumped from. In my entire life, I had never heard a dog howl like it. We all were convinced the dog had picked up his scent, and we had found David.

In that moment, my heart froze, I honestly could not believe that they had found him. It was a feeling more than disappointment when we checked the location out with the sonar equipment. It was not him and it turned out to be a rather large boulder. My heart did not want to believe it, so they checked it a few times. It was not him.

That evening, the sound of the howling dog would not leave my mind. It was as if the dog was crying and the sound went through my soul. Moments like this were painfully difficult, lots of tears were shed until we could muster up the energy to restart. But we couldn't give up, we would put on our armour and believe that tomorrow would be the day we would find him.

Struggling to Cope

Life just seemed so unfair and so cruel; David was gone, but he was also missing. I prayed, I begged, I promised, I would have done anything to find him - anything for this nightmare to come to an end.

I would often plead with David that we needed to find him. I felt angry that he had left me. I couldn't comprehend why we were all going through this on top of everything else. I felt like he owed it to us to, at least let us find him. I was a mess; I was struggling to sleep. I was not eating. Instead, I was living off the soft drink, Gatorade to get me through the day. I think it was pure choice, my life had been pulled from under me, so I was going to control anything else I could. Right now, the only things I felt like I had control over were eating and sleeping. Nobody could force me to do that.

On top of the control, I did not want to close my eyes as living in this nightmare was terrible enough, but waking up to it was incredibly realistic. It felt like I was reliving it over and over again.

We were becoming much busier at the lake. I realised I needed sleep to be an essential part of my routine. So, I went to the other side of the control issue and began sleeping too much when I realised that a little tablet would knock me out. I remember the first night taking one and it was like someone gave me solitude taking me away from the nightmare I was living.

Funny thing is, when I woke up, I had to face the cards I had been dealt. I thought back to when I would have heard a tragic story and how, at the time and even shortly after, it would have struck a chord with me. As life keeps on moving, it would have remained a distant memory, but I would have just got on with my life. It's different when it's your life. It consumes you, not even for a second would my mind switch off from what was going on.

The Clock was Ticking

We had now been at the lake for over a week and the weather was very warm, reaching over 30 degrees nearly every day. We were spending most of our days out on boats. I got accustomed to wearing life jackets, to the point I refused to take it off. I even wore it to bed. I could not explain it and I do not think anyone else understood. I felt secure when I had it on. It eased the pressure that was on my chest. My heart was often pounding and panic attacks were a regular occurrence. Somehow the life jacket offered me some comfort. It made me feel a little bit safer, knowing I could pull the strings tighter to provide an immediate effect or relief. Maybe there was a hidden meaning in the fact that a life jacket can prevent someone from drowning. To be honest, I was so vulnerable at that moment in time, I am not quite sure. All I do know was that I felt better with the life jacket on than without it.

I left that life jacket on for days even though everyone pleaded with me to take it off. I mentioned how hot the weather conditions were, but my body must have been in complete shock because I could not feel the heat at all. I am sure I looked a sight, but I didn't care. My physical exterior, as well as my interior body, was crumbling. Nothing mattered bar finding David. I felt so vulnerable. I had morphed into a childlike version of myself. I longed for someone to tell me it was going to be alright. Nobody could, or would do that because they knew all I wanted was David.

I was crying out for help and do not get me wrong; I could not have been anymore supported, but my whole being ached for David. I was quickly turning into a different version of myself, one I was not familiar with - a version of me who felt so far removed from society. I did not know how to cope with what was going on; I needed something, anything to ease the pain. Sometimes, the pain was so bad I would stare out onto the lake wondering should I just jump in too? Surely that would be easier than what was going on around me. I used to think David had it easy where he went to, rather than us, left trying to deal with this. Through it all, I never lost the fight in me to find David. The quote 'you do not know how strong you are until being strong is the only option you have got' always sticks in my head.

The longer we spent at the lake, the more of a shell of myself I became. I didn't know who this person was anymore. I just knew she was hanging on with a string which at any moment was going to break.

At this point, the search was escalating, and we had canine search teams and helicopters out every day on the lake searching for David. I'll never forget the first time going out in the helicopter. Up to this point, we were always searching on boats and this really came as a shock to the system seeing the vast landscape spread before us.

To get into the helicopter, we had to go to the helipad which was located on the grounds of a fancy hotel. Before this, I associated helicopters with excitement, but now I was very aware of what we were in the helicopter for. As we got ready to get into the helicopter, kids and families were watching on with pure joy and awe. If only they knew the reason why.

Up in the sky, looking down on the lake, I remember just crying it was so distressing. I knew the lake was big, but to see it from up there, it was surreal, David could have been anywhere. Literally, anywhere. The lake was colossal with no end in sight. I didn't like the helicopter, I found it too disheartening. I stuck to searching on the boat instead. Another part of me thought I would be too far away if we found David.

On the boat, I was near the water. I believed that when we found David, I would be present. I had this vision like something from the movies that I would be on the boat. I would be with him and mind him. The helicopter was not going to work for me at all.

We had the best professional support, but we were still nowhere closer to finding David. My heart ached and I longed to see him, but then I also longed to stay at the lake forever searching for him because then I could avoid reality for another while.

I was so determined and focused on finding David that I just got stuff done, not knowing how my body was functioning at all. The situation really did get the better of me at times. I just needed to be far away from everything. I told you before about the little magic sleeping tablets; I say magic because that is what they felt like to me. You could buy them over the counter in Canada, and I made sure I had my very own stash. Sleeping was the only thing that gave me a break from this nightmare until, of course, I woke up. I was being tested in every way imaginable. We all were. Yet, an inner resilience always guided and pushed us on to be strong.

Light Through the Darkness

In the early days, it was beyond hard and I fully believe David was pushing us on because I do not know how else we did it. As I reflect and write this book, it was noticeably clear that this journey we were on was divinely guided.

On the hardest of days at the lake or when we hit a lull, someone else would come on board and fill us with hope. The most amazing people joined us on this journey and each one played a valuable part. It is like David handpicked every single person to walk this journey with us in some shape or form. It sounds unbelievable, but throughout the first few weeks at the lake, we even had moments of laughter and joy, which were also down to David.

I began to have such a love-hate relationship with the lake and its surroundings. The one thing I did know is that there was nowhere else I would rather have been. Some days I truly hated it, and on other days I started to grow fond of it. When the sun was shining, and the light was catching the reflection of the water, it was glorious. It was quite a majestic place and I could imagine David being in awe of its beautiful surroundings.

David's Paradise and Guiding him back with Music

One of David's last words before his accident was that this place 'is paradise'. For a long time, I could not see or understand this. Other times, I could see how mesmerising the lake was. It soothed my soul to know that David thought this place was paradise. The moments of comfort we got in the early days, unfortunately, seemed to be far outweighed by the overwhelming pain and grief. Sometimes, I just felt like I was being tortured.

I was in so much pain and agony, but I also had this slight feeling something more was going on. David's life could not just end so abruptly for no reason. I questioned everything; 'would this have happened if he stayed in Vancouver?' I harboured guilt 'why did I let him go?' I simply did not have time to get stuck in the mental trap that was becoming my mind.

We needed to find David, and we were going to do everything to make this a possibility. We were all stepping up to the challenge and showing qualities and traits we did not even know we had. We were going to find him even if it broke us in the process, so be it. It sounds all doom and gloom and, trust me, it mostly was. Amid the darkness, amazing synchronicities started to happen and began to spread some light within the darkness.

David was gone in the physical sense, but it became clear that he was, somehow, guiding this journey to find him. I cannot describe it but sometimes being near the lake, I felt his presence so strong. I often longed to be by myself near the water so I could spend time with him and talk to him.

The previous Christmas before we went to Canada, I had bought him a speaker that you could play music from in the shower. He was chuffed with himself. David was big into gadgets and technology and even got the nickname 'Gadget Gav' over the years. I used to sneak off and find a quiet place to be near the water alone. I would play David's playlist to him by putting the speaker into the water. It brought me some comfort, and I felt close to him like he was listening. I often prayed the music would bring him closer to us. I was willing to give anything a go.

The Dragonfly

The first big sign we got from David blew my mind away. I cannot even remember what day it was; time and days were irrelevant at the lake. I remember it being around the afternoon as the group were gathered up around the campervan. David's sister and I were sitting on the bridge which was a common occurrence. We all did this a few times a day. I would often sit and stare out into the lake, wondering how my life came to this and pleading with David or whoever was up there that today was the day. Today, we would find David or get some positive news.

On this day, we saw the most beautiful blue dragonfly. Now, I had seen dragonflies before, they were everywhere. Quickly, it became apparent that there was something different about this one. It wanted to stay around. It was as if it was saying 'hello' to us.

Anyone reading this who knows anything about dragonflies will know they are quick, and it would not be easy to catch them. But, not this one. This one just wanted to hang around which was quite unusual. We went over to try and catch it, thinking it would fly away, but it didn't. We even managed to put it onto a little stick. If anyone had seen us, I'm sure we looked strange conversing with a dragonfly on a stick. It was much more than just the dragonfly because it sparked a feeling of peace and comfort within us. It was a sign. David had sent us a sign.

That little dragonfly stayed on that stick while we walked from the bridge to the campervan to show him to the others. I think everyone thought it was a little strange. There was nothing keeping that dragonfly there and it could have flown away at any time, but it did not. I even managed to get a picture of it.

After everyone got a look at the dragonfly and listen to me excitingly tell everyone it was a sign from David, the dragonfly flew off and went on its merry way. I did not know what the dragonfly meant, but I knew it meant something.

That dragonfly was blue, such a symbolic colour for David, as it was his GAA club colours in Ireland.

Later that day, someone showed me a quote about dragonflies, and what they symbolise. The quote read:

"Legend has it that dragonflies were given an extra set of wings so that angels could ride on their back, smaller than small, yet whenever you see a winged masterpiece, you can be certain that an angel has come down from heaven to visit you".

My heart felt heavy, but I also felt so uplifted. I knew it was David and now I had proof. I remember wanting to tell everyone, which I did. They could all see it sparked something within me. How amazing was this? Was David showing us signs to help guide us?

In some peculiar way, it stirred an excitement in me. If he can do that what else can he show us?

This was only the beginning. I was going to keep asking David for signs to see what I would get. David was not with us physically, but I knew after seeing the dragonfly he was so much closer to us; we just could not see him.

That evening, I googled searched dragonflies and what they symbolised. I came across the most beautiful poem, which touched me right to my core. I think it is so symbolic it earned a place in this book.

"Once, in a little pond, in the muddy water under the lily pads, there lived a small water beetle in a community of water beetles. They lived a simple and comfortable life in the pond with few disturbances and interruptions.

Once in a while, sadness would come to the community when one of their fellow beetles would climb the stem of a lily pad and would never be seen again. They knew when this happened; their friend was dead, gone forever.

Then, one day, one little water beetle felt an irresistible urge to climb up that stem. However, he was determined that he would not leave forever. He would come back and tell his friends what he had found at the top.

When he reached the top and climbed out of the water onto the surface of the lily pad, he was so tired, and the sun felt so warm, that he decided he must take a nap. As he slept, his body changed and when he woke up, he had turned into a beautiful blue-tailed dragonfly with broad wings and a slender body designed for flying.

So, fly he did! And, as he soared, he saw the beauty of a whole new world and a far superior way of life to what he had never known existed.

Then, he remembered his beetle friends, and how they were thinking by now, he was dead. He wanted to go back to tell them and explain to them that he was now more alive than he had ever been before. His life had been fulfilled rather than ended. But his new body would not go down into the water. He could not get back to tell his friends the good news. Then he understood that their time would come when they, too, would know what he now knew. So, he raised his wings and flew off into his joyous new life!"

- Author Unknown

I remember reading this repeatedly with tears streaming down my face. David was trying to tell us he was now at peace, that he was gone to his eternal home. After the initial feeling of sadness this brought, I began to feel some relief. David was ok, and wherever he was, it was beautiful. And just like that, my obsession with dragonflies started. Whenever I saw dragonflies, I knew it was David saying over and out, 'I am here guiding you'.

More Signs

I had got a glimpse of how uplifting and powerful the signs that David sent us could be. I remember one day we were out on a boat searching for David, we still had all the search teams out daily and every resource that we possibly needed. It was all hands-on deck, but unfortunately, we were still no closer to finding him. By now, it was becoming overwhelming and I recall being on the boat with a pair of binoculars in my hand searching the lake. This was starting to feel more normal than abnormal. All of us on the boat would be patiently on the lookout for anything symbolic. Anything at all!

Sometimes, the frustrations would kick in, mostly when you felt like you were going around in circles. I remember asking David for a sign, closing my eyes, pleading, waiting and, yet nothing. In my head, I got annoyed we had now been here for weeks and it was beginning to feel like we were being punished.

Suddenly, Justin Timberlake's song, 'Cry Me A River' began to float into my head, the lyrics kept repeating to the point I had no other option but to listen to them.

'Cry Me a River' sounded ironic as I was doing just that daily, endlessly. I remember thinking this is pointless. 'Why could David not give me a sign I could understand?' Everyone else on the boat was completely oblivious that I was at war with my head and David. Then suddenly, I started repeating the words, Justin, Timber....lake. It took me a little while to get over my annoyance with Justin Timberlake's soundtrack in my head.

As I repeated the words for what felt like the 100th time, Justin Timberlake, I got the message. David was trying to tell us he was 'just in timber lake'. He was stuck; he was trying to tell us he was stuck. I remember getting off the boat with a strut in my step like I had won at Trivial Pursuit. This meant so much more to me than the words. It showed me David was listening to me. All I had to do was play ball and listen to him too. I just kept saying, 'Justin Timberlake'.

I told everyone I asked David for a sign, and that is what he gave me. I was speaking so fast as I knew I was onto something. Everyone looked at me in disbelief. Of course, David was stuck in the lake; we all knew that. I was so focused on the fact that it was a sign from him more than anything else. They continued to engage with me, but I felt they did not feel the same excitement I felt. David was communicating with us and giving us signs. I think they were, however, delighted that it gave me hope and a bit of a pep in my step.

The feeling I got was enough; I didn't need anyone else's reassurance or belief. I didn't care, I knew it was David, and it gave me great strength and comfort. That is the thing about signs that are meant for you. Your loved ones in spirit do not need to prove to you that they are around. They send the signs. It is up to you if you are receptive to them. There is no logic to the signs we are sent. I believe it is all about faith and trust. I just had to let go of all my judgments and put my full faith and trust in knowing that these signs were from David.

The feeling you get when you surrender your resistance to signs is so enchanting.

The closest thing I can describe it to is feeling a warm embrace around your heart. After that, I remember asking David for signs all the time, and always, he sent something symbolic so that I knew it was him. Each sign I got, gave me that little bit more hope and courage to push on.

Going Home

Severe anxiety was kicking in as it had been suggested that it might be time to return to Ireland and hold a memorial ceremony for David. By now, we had been at the lake for over two weeks. I was adamant I was not going home to Ireland. I didn't understand why we should go home when we hadn't found David. To leave the lake without David felt wrong on so many levels to me. It felt like I would have been doing him an injustice or failing him.

Sometimes, I wondered would I ever leave the lake until we found him? If anything, in the last few weeks, I had got into a routine. I had become accustomed to the lake and all its quirks. It was the closest thing I knew to normal even though it was not one bit normal at all.

We had a focus at the lake; every day was another day we could find David and that was a reason to get up. I had the same attitude daily - today's the day. Do not get me wrong at the end of each day searching it was very disheartening to think we were not successful. But in my head, I had to believe that anything was possible.

What if they found him and we were in Ireland? For days, it was just so much easier to say 'no'. Reflecting, I was terrified. I knew at the lake I had created my safety blanket. Ireland was going to whip my blanket away, and it was going to strike me that David was really gone.

After a lot of encouragement and discussion, I very reluctantly and unhappily agreed to go back to

Ireland for a short period. A strict plan with people we trusted would ensure services would remain at the lake searching for David. The days leading up to our departure were filled with extreme anxiety for me. I didn't know if I would be able for the reality to hit me.

The journey back to Ireland was painful, with all of us individually just mentally trying to prepare ourselves. As I sat on the plane, I remembered my last journey when David and I started our new adventure and I shed a few tears. It hit me how naïve I had been most of my life. I just assumed people on planes were happy because clearly, they were all going on holiday. I remember looking around at our group, and we were indeed not happy. We were heartbroken and traumatised.

Landing into Dublin Airport was so challenging and surreal. It felt like the walls were about to fall in on me. This was where we had started our adventure, heading to Vancouver to start our new life. Here I was, back again this time 'by myself'. I think it was the first time it hit me that I was truly by myself, not a 'couple' anymore. It was just me. I had been with David for what felt like all my life. I would often forget about the signs he sent me, when I felt like this, and I felt so isolated and alone.

I didn't know how to function without him, never mind go home, and hold a memorial service for him. What even was a memorial service? Everything that was going on was feeling so surreal. We had no coffin, no David, and my mind was in a lost loop of 'what ifs'. In those particular days, my little bit of spirituality dwindled. The signs I had been sent were now a distant memory. Instead, I had to just focus on doing what I needed to do to return to the lake.

When I arrived back in Mayo, I first met with family and friends. Everyone was heartbroken. Family and friends held me in a way I had never felt before. It was not just me in pain; everyone was hurting. David, in such a short lifetime, had touched so many people's hearts. It was so comforting, but with every hug I received, my heart just broke more, and more. I couldn't just feel my own broken heart anymore; I could feel everyone else's.

Sorry for Your Loss

People travelled the length and breadth of the country to sympathise. My hand was sore from all the handshakes, and my shoulders were aching from all the firm hugs filled with people's despair of what was going on. Everyone wondering the same thing, 'Were we going to find David?' Strangers hugged me like they had known me all my life. In every hug, I felt their pain for us. Their despair at what we were going through. I felt numb; at times, I did not know how I felt. All I knew was that it was beyond awful. I kept wishing for this horrendous feeling to go away. I knew, that was not going to happen unless we found David alive and well, and I could go back to my everyday life. And then there were 'those words'. Those words we are programmed to say at funerals, "I'm sorry for your loss".

Each time I heard those words, my heart sunk further and further and I longed for them to say anything else. I stood there and shook hands until my hands felt numb, just like the rest of me. The words continuing to float around in my head, 'sorry for your loss'. The only person I wanted a hug from was David. I needed him; this was terribly hard. Being at the lake was hard, but this was so, so much harder.

Needing to be Back at the Lake & Reality Sinking In

After the memorial service, we spent a few more days in Ireland. Our days consisted of checking in with the crew at the lake to see were there any updates? The days started to drag here, and the bleakness of the situation became more apparent.

People would ask us about the lake, and we would show them pictures and fill them in. The lake was so vast that unless you were out there it was hard to explain exactly what we were dealing with - a monster of a lake with incredibly challenging conditions. It started to become even more frustrating having those conversations, as the problematic situation we were in would hit home. My mind would flicker back to being up in the helicopter and seeing what we were dealing with in terms of the physical vastness of the lake and surrounding area. David could have been anywhere in that lake, and that was the really scary part.

I remember one day being informed that if David's body surfaced overnight there was a chance that a bear or some other animal could find him first. I had so much else to think about; I was not going to let my mind try and process that information. Instead, for now, that was planted as far at the back of my mind as I possibly could put it.

We were also realising that the water conditions were becoming a lot worse than we expected adding another dynamic to us finding David and bringing him home. There was a glacier runoff and the water conditions underneath were cloudy, which made the vision for diving nearly impossible and dangerous.

Being at home, we had time to sit down and process what we were dealing with. It was not looking hopeful. We needed to go back with the same attitude we left with. Ok, the conditions were up against us, but we had hope and David on our side. We also had the prayers and support from so many people. Everyone had the same common goal - that we would find David and bring him home.

The days at home were exceedingly difficult, but somehow, we managed to stumble through them. Soon it was time to return to the lake to continue the search. I was ready; I needed to be back by the water. I needed to feel close to David.

Round Two & Returning to Vancouver

We had come up with a plan that we should spend a few days in Vancouver before making the journey to the lake. Even landing in Canada was enough for me, I felt so much closer to David knowing I was in the same country as the lake. I had not prepared myself for the intense feelings that being back in Vancouver would bring to me. I was so focused on getting out of Ireland and getting to the lake that I do not think I had given it a second thought.

Vancouver did not feel safe anymore. The place we had called our home for the last few months was not our home anymore. Nowhere was 'home' without David. Everywhere I went, I carried the same feeling that David was no longer going to be in any of the places I went to, and that hurt so bad and made me feel so hollow.

With all the strength I had, I spent one day showing David's parents our local hangout spots in Vancouver. I walked around that day with a heavy heart. Each place that held a memory now had a heartache. I tried to be strong as David's parents' hearts were breaking as much as mine. Looking back, I wonder, were we just adding more pain? We even went and walked up to the apartment we used to live in. Staring up at our apartment where we started our blissful adventure, it became evident it was not our apartment anymore. Someone had moved into it. I wondered who they were and were they as happy as we were in that apartment.

We then went to the beach where we had spent endless days. We traced the footprints David and I used to make without a care in the world, not knowing that the life we knew was going to change in an instant. If we knew would we have done anything different? What would it have been like to know? My mind needed a break from all these questions; it needed answers too. All I knew was that I wanted to know right now, 'where was David?'

Reflecting, I do not know how we all got the strength even to do that. I knew, the sooner we got out of Vancouver, the quicker we got to the lake. The determination and strength I had for that would have pulled me through anything. Also, David was with us, giving us strength and pulling us along. The most beautiful thing through all this was the bond I had cemented with David's family. We held each other together like glue. In all the challenges and difficult situations, we had together, the love we had for each other was so strong.

In them, I saw David, and in me, they had their little piece of him. A beautiful relationship blossomed because of the love we all shared for him. We grew comfort from each other, we shared the same love and now shared the same pain. The more time I spent with them, I could see why David was such a beautiful person. He, indeed, was that person because of who he was reared by. In this, they had taken me on, the good and the bad, and I was truly touched and blessed by this.

In Vancouver, I had time to think before returning to the lake. I often wondered had David planned it all to work out this way to give us a focus and keep our minds busy. Is that why we had not found him yet?

I was broken, yet I was so determined and focused on finding him. I did not have time to sit and wallow in my grief. I had to keep pushing on, moving forward. I somehow could see he needed to give us a focus, and for some strange reason, I knew everything was as it was supposed to be. There was some kind of reason as to why we had not found him already. I couldn't put my finger on it, but I felt guided to look deeper into what was going on. Even the fact that we were back in Vancouver, must have had an explanation.

Time to Return to the Lake

It was eventually time to return to the lake. We were now even more determined that we were going to find David. We were under no illusions and were all too aware that time was not on our side. We only had a small gap of time before the weather conditions made it impossible for us to continue our search. That didn't stop us, and we were returning with the same attitude as before - 'today will be the day we find him'.

Nothing had changed since we left Ireland. Search teams continued to scan the lake every day, searching for David. We also had helicopters out daily monitoring the area. Unfortunately, we had not made any advancements or received any positive news. We had to go with the positives. At least, we had not found out that a wild animal had come across him. As I type, it sounds surreal, but such were the odds we were up against. We had to take any positive we could get.

Returning to the lake, we were filled with so much anxiety as we knew if we were not successful this time in finding David, we would have to return in the spring of 2018. The thought of that made me feel sick - a whole seven months waiting to return to the lake._My mind couldn't focus on that. The thought of it made my insides scramble. This was not an option in my eyes. We were going to find him.

I cannot explain, but I felt braver than the last time being at the lake. Our situation had changed too with everyone knowing we only had a short period to search. It also was not as daunting the second time around going to the lake. I had an attitude that I would have done anything to make finding David happen.

I think a lot of people were afraid my expectations were too high. That I would not cope if things didn't plan out the way I expected. I was completely and utterly convinced that we were going to find David this time around.

It Was Like We Never Left

Arriving at the lake, it felt like we never left. I walked straight over to the bridge and stared out over at the water. All the emotions came rushing back, but that determination prevailed. I took a deep breath saying to myself, 'I have this, we are going to find David, or I am going to die trying'.

The campsite was now quite different. It was less busy, as peak season was over, which was nice. It was so lovely to connect and thank the people who had kept the show running while we were gone. We could not thank them enough; they eased our anxiety, knowing that, in our absence every effort was being made to find David. The professionals had at this stage secured an ROV- a remotely operated underwater vehicle. An underwater robot as I used to call it.

I remember thinking that David would have been looking down at all this equipment in awe. He loved technology and gadgets so much. It was like he had planned it all so he could look down and see all the equipment in action.

We also had the canine search team back to join us and professional dive teams who scanned the area to try and find David's body, it was 'all systems go'. The one positive about this time was that we got to be even more involved than before. I remember one day being asked to go out on the boat with one of the search dogs. I had only seen them work from a distance before, and I was fascinated. I got to sit at the back of the boat, holding a GPS. If the dog pinpointed anything of significance, I would be given the alert by their handler.

Afterwards, the dog handler would go over the coordinates, and if they thought there was anything significant, we would use the sonar equipment to check it out.

It was so amazing to see the dogs at work. They were trained by scent to help locate missing people. I was genuinely grateful to the people who were sent to help us. They were so professional and sensitive; they were dealing with people who were heartbroken and very fragile. We also got to watch as they put the ROV into the water. The ROV was hooked up to a camera, and it could scan the water while we watched on from a screen up above.

The conditions, however, were not at all ideal for the ROV as the water was very cloudy and, eventually, after a few days, we had to discontinue this. It was disheartening, but there was nothing we could do. We continued to use the sonar equipment to scan the water, but we were not picking up anything of significance. I continued to remain positive, but I was slowly starting to realise with every day that passed, we were a day closer to having to leave and go home. This time, going home would be different. It meant going home and not returning for several months.

I found the weeks after the memorial service extremely difficult. 'How would I manage a few months?' At this stage, I did not even know where my home was. David and I had our home in Vancouver, but in all the chaos, I had no option but to move out of our apartment. It looked like my only option was to return home to Ireland and move back in with my family. I was not in any fit state to return to work. In that moment, my life was put on pause until David was found and we brought him home. I would find David, and then I would deal with what was to come next.

Nobody Could Take My Hope Away

When everything seemed to be taken away from me, I knew nothing, or nobody could take my hope away. I was going to cling onto it with everything I had. Even if the signs showed differently. We were going to find him this time around. We had to.

Every day, our family and friends in Ireland eagerly awaited to hear how the day went. Every day sending that reply text saying 'not today' was soul-destroying, but I always tried to give people at home some hope as I wasn't giving up just yet.

I remember reading that fear is the opposite of love. I was petrified every day of what we were going through. The love I felt in my heart was so much stronger. I was able for anything even if it scared the life out of me. Love was going to push me through. In a weird way, finding David's body was so important that we did not have time to think about the fact that we were never going to see him again or that he was gone.

Time was dwindling on us and we all knew it, but nobody wanted to point out directly that we were coming to the end of the road. We had exhausted all avenues. Hearing the words 'not this time around' shattered my heart, we were going to have to go back to Ireland for the second time without David.

Unfortunately, there was nothing else we could do, but get ready to leave the lake. I had the utmost confidence in all the professionals who were helping us and I knew the dedication they had put in over the last few weeks. They would not advise us to leave if there was anything else we could have done to make the search successful.

The day we left the lake was just horrendous. Searching for David had become our new purpose. Finding David was our focus. For days, I knew this was coming, but I was not prepared for this. I did not want to leave. To me, it did not feel like saying 'bye', it felt like giving up. I remember saying sorry to David numerous times in my head. I felt so much guilt like we were letting him down. Deep down, I knew he was so proud of us. I missed him terribly and I was so afraid of going home. There was nothing I could do. I had to. I felt broken leaving the lake. The car was so quiet, and we all just cried. This time it was not meant to be, but it was not for the will of trying.

Vancouver Take Two

I could not consider the idea to return to Ireland just yet, so I went to Vancouver for a week before I returned to Ireland. This was my second time in Vancouver, and I assumed it might not be as difficult. How wrong I was. If grief had taught me anything, it had led me always to expect the unexpected. The second time around, I found it even more difficult. The reality was that after this I was going home to Ireland. I did not have a focus. I just had myself and a bucket full of emotions.

I was very aware of being in Vancouver by myself. Everywhere I went I saw and felt David, which hit me even more that he was gone. Everywhere I went; this overwhelming feeling would not leave me. I knew it was grief. I just wanted some reprieve.

I remember one day taking a stroll down by where we used to live. As I stared at my apartment, I envisioned my life three months ago. I would have done anything to be transported back then. We had so many happy memories, but every time I thought of them, it brought me such pain. I stared at my apartment and realised David was gone and my life in Vancouver was gone. I felt like a massive part of me was gone. Grief was a constant struggle and hard work.

On reflection, I was lost, not one single part of me did I recognise. I had so little control in my life; everything was falling apart, and there was nothing I could do about it. It is tough to describe grief, but sometimes I used to think this is going to kill me. In any given moment, I honestly did not know how I was going to feel. Once the intense emotions came, I realised very quickly it was easier to let them out rather than be like a pot that was going to boil over, or else I was going to explode. There was a constant strain and intense pressure over my heart. It was so intense that I often wondered was my heart physically as well as mentally broken.

Returning to Ireland Again

The week I spent in Vancouver before returning to Ireland, I longed to be back at the lake. I would have done anything to be there, even if it meant just sitting on the dock staring out onto the water. It pained me to be at the lake, yet it was the only place I wanted to be. I was so aware I was still in Canada, yet I always felt so far away from where I needed to be. The only thing I did know was that it was better than being in Ireland.

So many people in Vancouver surrounded me, but I still felt alone. I had called Vancouver my home, but it was no longer home. My home was with David, it did not matter where we were as long as we were together. David was gone, and I was homeless. I just wanted to be with him; my heart just ached for him. I just needed one of his bear hugs and for him to mutter 'everything is going to be alright'.

The pain I felt was so intense and overbearing I wondered how I was going to make it through the next few months in Ireland. It was going to be such a drastic change. I feared the unknown, of what it would look like. Mostly, I feared leaving Canada again for the second time without David.

For now, I could not think of this and tried to push these thoughts to the back of my head. I had no choice. I had to go back to Ireland. I had got this far not knowing where I got the strength, it had to be David pushing me and guiding me on. I felt so weak, broken, and empty, yet at times so strong, brave, and determined. It felt like a higher force, something I did not fully understand or could not explain was giving me the strength and pushing me on. I knew I had to keep the faith and keep talking and praying to David. I think that is what scared me the most. I was so afraid that when I returned to Ireland, that I would lose my faith or hope that we would find David. I was afraid I would lose my purpose to get up every day, that I would lose myself a little bit more than I already had.

David Sent Me Hope

The journey from Canada back to Ireland was as heartbreaking as the last time. This time, it would not be a few weeks before we returned, it could be up to 7 months. Nothing could ease the pain of that, nothing. The only thing that loosened the blow a little was the fact I had made this journey before. My faith and heart believed this would be the last occasion; we would fly back to Ireland without David. I also had a distraction; I was going to meet my new puppy.

Landing into Knock Airport was extremely difficult. I have got the post-holiday blues before, but this feeling was something so much bigger than that. I walked out the doors of the airport and felt the cold air hit my face. I wanted to cry as I was so tired and jet-lagged.

It was an escape and distraction from my inner chaotic mind to see my friend standing there holding this fluffy bundle of joy, who I was to name, Hope. I stood outside the door of the airport, cuddling my new puppy. I couldn't explain it, but I knew she had been sent to me and was somehow going to help me. I could sense the innocence and vulnerability of Hope. Hope didn't know my life had fallen apart; she was not going to judge me or feel sorry for me; she was just going to love me unconditionally.

Arriving home, the moment I had been dreading the last few weeks was not so bad after all. I was so distracted by this tiny, adorable little puppy that needed me. I was very aware that for the next seven months I would remain here, back living at home. But for now, I did not need to think of that. I needed to get Hope settled into her new surroundings.

That evening, I think everyone was delighted to welcome Hope into the family. It gave us all something to focus on rather than the obvious. Instead of focusing on what we had not accomplished or discuss the intense pain we were all in, we all sat and stared at Hope. Hope brought us moments of joy and even brought a smile to our faces. It was an excellent distraction for the first few days, and I relished in minding her. Hope knew not of my intense pain, Hope needed me in a world where I felt genuinely hopeless, as ironic as that sounds.

Reality set in a few days later, it was apparent we were back in Ireland, and the search for David had ceased for the next few months. I felt deflated; I wanted to stay in bed, curtains closed to stop the light getting in. All I wanted to do was avoid the noise of the outside world.

I knew that Hope needed me, and something stronger in me made myself get up. It could have been my conscience kicking in. My faith led me to believe it was David pulling strings from up above. I knew staying in bed was not going to make me feel any better. David knew me better than anyone else; he knew I always needed a focus and that I loved looking after people. David was going to make sure somehow, I would have some reason to get up in the morning and right now it was Hope.

Trying to Survive

I think I consciously decided that eating, sleeping and looking after Hope were the only things on my priority list. My main priority was to find David, but that was put on standstill for the next few months. Not a second went by that I did not think about him or the lake. My mind pondered what the lake looked like. Was David's body still there?

Grief took centre stage in my life and showed up in full force. I realised quickly that grief was sporadic and unreliable; it popped up when I least expected it. My life had turned into a roller coaster of emotions. I quickly got fed up with trying to ride the waves of the storm. The more I tried to control the grief, the less control I had over it. It had this talent in always taking me by surprise; it would sweep in over me like a shadow.

Sometimes, my mind pretended David was not dead at all. We did not have a funeral, a coffin, a burial all the things I associated with someone dying. How could he be dead? We needed to find David to bring him home and bury him. We needed to make all this feel real. Grief became my best friend and a daily occurrence in my life. A friend you really would rather not hang out with, but at the same time, they are familiar. Grief was very needy; it did not give me any space to breathe at all. It got annoyed if I did not provide it with time, and if I tried to ignore it, it would just come back fighting stronger and louder. I was lost, at least at the lake, I had a focus, here I had nothing. Everywhere I went lay constant reminders to the fact that David was gone. Life felt so unfair, and I just kept being reminded of it. Grief was consuming me; Over and over repeatedly, I wondered where David was, when and where were we going to find him?

David Was Alone, and I Felt Guilty

I felt so guilty. I was doing nothing to help find David. Deep in my soul, I knew there was nothing I could do. My hands were tied. Even if I went back to Canada, I could not get down to the lake as the road was now impassable due to the severe weather conditions. That did not shake my unnerving feeling of guilt that riddled me. If anything, it added to it. David was all alone, and nobody would be near the lake for months.

This anxiety often brought up feelings of anger. Anger at the situation I was currently in. Anger we had not found him. Wrath of the life that had just been robbed from me. All I could do was cry. Tears that wept from a sad and weary soul, tears that tried to keep the faith and be hopeful but often felt so hopeless. I felt like I was letting David down. He was the one person I loved and cared about more than anyone on this planet.

I never really understood before what it meant when something you love is taken from you. I had watched movies about it. I never thought for a second, something like this would happen to me. David was more than my something, he was my someone, the only one I wanted, needed and he was gone, and every day it was hitting me more and more.

Being back in Ireland, the cracks were starting to show. It was hitting me how broken I had become. The only thing keeping me going had now also been taken away from me. From being so actively engaged and focused in searching for David, to having nothing to do bar think. It was very apparent that I was not ok. I had more time to actively think about what was going on and the situation I had been placed in—the one thing I did not want to do.

My patience was running thin, but that was the only thing I needed. Patience to remain hopeful for the next few months until I could return to the lake to find David. I was struggling with the concept of time and waiting. It now felt like David was teaching me life skills and up first was patience, followed by faith. I had no choice but to remain patient; there was nothing else I could do. I also had to keep my faith in the unknown, faith that against all the odds, everything would work out. Even if at times I did not believe it, I had to keep my faith.

Anything to Get Through the Day

I lived to get through the day, just to face another one again and often wondered, would I ever feel any satisfaction or joy in my life again? Every day was a struggle, and I often wished not to be here. The pain was just so overwhelming. I had never cried like this before; each tear was of extreme loss and sadness. If my tears had words, they would have said "Put me down". I felt like a wounded animal that was in so much agony and pain wanting someone to take some of the pain away. I never had in my life experienced pain like this; it was so horrendous, and the worse thing was it was not going away or getting any easier.

I quickly realised nobody was going to put me down or take any of my pain away. I needed some release; anything to make this easier. Sleeping tablets became my saving grace, and night time became my favourite part of the day. I knew the sleeping tablets would aid me to having a few hours rest from this nightmare. In my eyes, it was like turning on an 'off' button to my life for a short while. I was also crippled with anxiety, so I had a supply of Xanax that I would frequently use to get me through the day. I needed something, anything to take the edge off of life for a little bit. I don't condone this and reflecting now I wish I could have managed my emotions more and not needed the medication. But I was struggling to cope and even to just survive. I needed anything to help ease the pain. I would retreat to bed as early as possible and then sleep in as late as I could. My aim was to make the day as short and tolerable as it could be. Typical daily routine things annoyed me; I would get frustrated to hear people give out about minor things. I just could not understand how everyone was getting on with their lives when David was still missing.

My Outer Exterior Matching My Inner Exterior

I was starting to look exactly how I felt. I was frustrated that I had so little control over my life and realised dyeing my hair was one thing I could control. I began dyeing my hair, any chance I could get. I felt awful on the inside, so I picked colours that matched precisely how I felt. I went from having a lovely blonde hair colour to, at one stage, having nearly jet-black hair. Thinking back, maybe I intended to make my outside exterior reflect what I was feeling on the inside. I had lost my purpose, my reason for being. I had lost the love of my life, my partner of 10 years. My life had fallen to absolute pieces right before my very eyes. I did not know who I was. I had completely lost my identity. What scared me the most was that I didn't care who I was.

I was so angry David was gone and had left me. I was angry and resentful that everyone else's life was able to move on when mine was very clearly on pause. I was frustrated that we had not found David yet. Grief amplified every emotion, and it made me feel crushed and devastated. I just felt like a big ball of different emotions, and yet on other days, I felt absolutely nothing. I was numb to the core. I felt nothing. I was empty, a big ball of nothingness.

I preferred feeling numb, but I knew I always got some release going through all the chaotic emotions, even if at the time it felt hard and uncomfortable. All these emotions served a purpose whether I liked it or not. I was feeling angry because I was angry. I was feeling anxious because I was panicking, and I was nervous. The emotions felt so intense, and I often felt abnormal, when really, they were a very normal reaction to what had just happened. I started counselling as an added support and this helped me understand that all these feelings were ok; it was the intensity of them that was overbearing.

It all Got Too Much

One day, I remember feeling so much worse than any other day. I was sitting down in the kitchen watching Dr. Phil on TV, a common occurrence in my daily routine. I liked Dr. Phil because it made me feel like my situation could have been worse, listening to some of the life stories. It would get me out of my bubble; I was not the only one going through something difficult in their life.

That day, I felt so sad and lonely more intensely than any other day. I kept looking at the clock while watching the TV. I honestly felt that time was not moving at all. The feeling of dread started to set in. I had just woken up, but all I wanted to do was go back to bed again. I stared at the clock again, and panic struck. I knew today was going to be hard. I tried to put my focus back onto Dr. Phil, but even he could not distract my mind on that day. There was just a big dark cloud over me, and I just could not shake it. I knew there was no point saying it to anyone, as what could they do? I could not even really describe what was going on for me.

When it got that bad my only other way out was to go to sleep and try to switch my mind off yet it was too early for that. I remember pacing the kitchen, holding my two temples in despair. It was all just getting too much. I needed this feeling to go away, this dark cloud to lift. I remember going upstairs and sitting on my bed. I felt hopeless and needed this feeling to go away, quickly.

I knew in a drawer that I had a full box of antihistamines. I didn't even think about it; I just took the box and sat on my bed and popped one tablet after another tablet into my mouth. I needed to shake the dreaded feeling I had, and I did not care what happened.

I felt so irrational. I knew what I was doing, but I did not understand why.

Afterwards, I sat on my bed and cried. It only took me a few minutes to regret what I had done. I ran straight into the bathroom. I stuck my fingers down my throat and made myself get sick. I sat in a heap in the bathroom clung to the toilet seat, and I just cried and cried. I was so upset and angry at myself. I felt ashamed of what I had done. I could have kept what I had done to myself, but part of me felt afraid. Even though I had made myself sick, I was scared of the implications of my actions. I decided I would tell my Mum who was in the house at the time.

I proceeded to cry as I told her. She didn't know how to react which I was not surprised about. I tried to explain to her how I felt beforehand. I knew there was no point; I barely understood myself. Mum didn't know what to do so she called my friends who were nurses. They called out to the house and stayed with me for the evening. I knew everyone was already worried about me, and this would only have added to that.

For a long time, I was so ashamed. Indeed, I was going to leave it out of the book, but I think it accurately portrays how lost and low I felt for such a long time.

After that incident, I was linked in with the mental health community services and was put on antidepressants to help with my low mood. I needed this support at the time, and I am so grateful for this. It is so essential if you are struggling to seek out help. Along with these added supports, I was still attending counselling weekly. I highly recommend to anyone struggling never to be afraid to reach out and avail of different support services. The worst thing you can do is try to manage your emotions yourself, which can lead to you becoming overwhelmed.

With all the supports I received, I was able to put more of a routine into my life._This also helped me normalise all the emotions I was experiencing. I also started to get my focus and my faith back. I started asking David for signs again. I needed to know everything was going to be alright. I know that David did not stop sending me signs or making his presence known. I was just not in the mind-frame to notice them. I believe now I needed to go into an even darker place to regain some light into my life again.

From there on, I told myself I would just take each moment as it arises, and approach one day at a time. I wondered if everyone felt like this who experienced grief. I struggled to explain or articulate the words to describe how I was feeling. In one way, grief fascinated me. It was like being trapped at sea, so lost alone and afraid and then out of nowhere giant waves would come crashing in. Grief was making my physical body and mental health weak and tired. I was doing minimal physical activity, yet I felt like I had run a marathon when my most significant achievement on that day was getting out of bed.

I watched others around me who were also grieving for David. We had the same loss, the same pain, yet their grief was different and individual to them. It became apparent to me that grief is a very personal journey. I began to research grief and try to get some information on how to navigate it. Little did I know back then that all the answers I needed were within me. I was waiting for someone else to come and fix this for me. I would have done anything for someone to wave a magic wand over me and give me peace of mind and comfort.

Letting Myself See the Signs

Some days, I was so receptive and aware of the signs. I would be out walking, and a little robin would follow me, hopping along beside me. I would watch and be in awe of this beautiful bird knowing David had sent it to me, sending a rush of energy and comfort around my heart generally at the exact time I needed it. I just had this intuitive knowing that he had sent me the robin as a sign. I watched on lovingly as the little robin would fly in front of me like it was guiding me along.

Sometimes, I would try and take a picture of the majestic bird. Ironically, the robin would never hang around for a photo. This would give me a giggle; David was never fond of pictures and was always telling me off when I would try to get one with him. Every time I tried to get a photo and was close to getting one, the robin would fly away. As this made me laugh, I felt David looking down laughing too. I could imagine him joking about me not being able to get a photo with him.

David had a way of sending signs exactly when I needed them. When I was receptive to noticing them, of course. One day, I remember feeling so lonely, the grief cloud was starting to smother me and take over. I needed some release and a chance to breathe. I decided to go for a walk, to spend time in nature as it can be so healing. I instantly felt uplifted; I could feel his presence all around me. A similarity in the feeling I got with all the signs he sent me. A comforting feeling, one with no logic or reasoning whatsoever. A sense of intense love and rush to your heart. I could not see David, but I just knew it was him sending me all these signs to guide me and push me on. With each sign, I felt this feeling; it gave me a push to open my eyes and continue to look for the next sign he would send. With all the pain and suffering I was going through; I knew I liked this feeling.

After this beautiful, blissful moment in nature, I wrote a poem to express what I felt.

Today as I was missing you,

I did not know just what to do,

I decided to go for a walk,

To reminisce with you and talk.

Soon enough I knew that you were there,

In the wind, the trees, the air.

On its wings, I saw a butterfly,

Down from heaven, I said 'hi' It made me smile and cry.

Next, a dragonfly stopped by, I said hello and watched it go to and fro.

Then a robin plopped along, I wished it well, and it chirped along,

Soon enough, I was not sad. Instead, I felt love, and I felt glad,

All the signs you sent from above, it made my heart fill up with love, I know that you are always there, In the wind, the trees, the air.

I never thought of myself as a writer, but I felt so inspired to write that poem. It was like my soul needed to write it and that it came from a deeper place within me. On that day, David sent me each one of those animals. My heart nearly exploded with joy. David knew I needed a pick me up, and that is precisely what he did. I felt so low, leaving the house. I remember nearly skipping back to the house. I just wanted to tell the world that our loved ones are with us always. An inner knowing told me not to, not just yet.

No one else mattered in that moment David had sent me the signs. In a world where we need logic to back up everything, I did not. It was the feeling I got when I knew he had sent me signs. It was like a warm bubbly feeling all around me. I could have been resistant to them, but I knew deep in my soul it was him. I felt so invigorated, so alive. David was with me, and it could not have been any clearer.

He didn't just use nature or send animals as signs; he also sent people. We had a beautiful tree planted in his memory, and I would often go up there with the dogs. One day as I was sitting on David's bench looking out at his tree, a man approached me and asked me could he sit down. At the time, I was not really feeling anyone's company, but I didn't want to be rude, and I was not going to say 'no'. So, I replied 'yes', and as he sat down, we engaged in a conversation. He proceeded to tell me how he comes to the tree often to pray that David is found. I did not mention I was David's partner, and I asked him did he know David? He said he didn't, and this truly touched my heart. As a stranger, he was affected by David's story and even said he felt like he knew him. I could just tell this man was a gentle and kind soul. In that moment as we sat at the tree, I knew David had sent him. I felt the same feeling I mentioned before. This feeling began to spark a new found faith in me—a belief in the unknown.

I felt uplifted, hopeful, and it encouraged me to keep going knowing David was with me every step of the way. There was something incredibly special about this man. After a while, I told him I was David's girlfriend. He empathised with me, most sincerely. He, too, was familiar with grief. He spoke about his faith and how it had and continues to get him through the difficult times in his life. With each word he spoke, I could feel his inner strength, and that gave me great inspiration for what I was going through. He asked me if he could sing me a song as the two of us sat at the bench and I said of course he could.

The song he sang was about remembering your loved ones who have passed on; he even put David's name in it. As I listened on, I felt David's presence so strong in my heart. The comfort I received from those few minutes was so touching. After that encounter, I felt excited like I knew David had sent that man to give me hope. I ended up forming a friendship with him. Looking back, it was a completely random act of kindness but also a divinely guided meeting. A reflection of that man's faith sparked something in me. I remember thinking 'I just need to keep the faith that everything will be alright'.

Another evening my Mum, David's Mum and I all went to this man's house for a visit. When we arrived, he opened the door with a burst of excitement. He told us that before we arrived, a robin had flown into his house and flew into his sitting-room. He said the robin flew around the sitting room in circles. He then told us the robin hit off a picture on the wall and that the picture was a framed poem titled, 'Footprints in the Sand'.

We were all in shock. David had kept a copy of that poem in his bedroom from when he was a child. That poem was so significant that we read it out at David's memorial mass. We all took this as a beautiful sign from David, again showing us his presence is all around us. There was so much synchronicity; I knew it was all David. Again, I got that feeling in my heart when I knew David was around or guiding me. We all joked that was David giving the house the once over before we landed. David also had a way of trying to bring humour back into our lives. As we all sat there laughing, it felt so special to feel David's presence all around us.

Messages from Heaven

The signs were all starting to flow, and I knew exactly why. I had faith, and I was open and ready to receive them. The grief had not gone anywhere unfortunately, but I had regained some momentum and focus back into my life.

I had now been on antidepressants for a few weeks, and they appeared to be taking the edge off life a little bit. I still longed for answers. I needed to know if we were going to find David. I just needed to feel close to him, and being at the lake seemed like the closest place. I got inquisitive, and I would have tried anything to be able to connect with him and get the answers I needed.

I remember years previous, one of my friends trying to convince me to go and see a Psychic Medium. At the time, I was too afraid and refused to go. This time my life was in a different predicament, this time I had nothing to lose, I had already lost everything anyway. They could not tell me anything bad, because the worst thing in the world had already happened to me.

I started regularly going to Psychic Mediums to seek the answers I needed. Often the first thing I would ask was if we were going to find David? Sometimes, I would say nothing; they would read my energy and the reaction I would get was "Something terrible has happened, hasn't it?"

Now that I have had several experiences with Psychic Mediums, I feel silly for having initially being fearful of them as they have such a magical gift. They can communicate with loved ones in spirit and hold that space and open the communication. Psychic Mediums are the channels to deliver these messages. They provide a safe space where you can communicate with your loved one. They are just people like the rest of us with a unique and beautiful gift that bridges the gap between us and spirit.

Some of the readings I received blew my mind away. Some things only David and I would have known. It was hard, and I would often cry through most of the readings. It ignited my faith in us being able to connect with our loved ones on a deeper level. The only question I ever needed answered was 'are we going to find him?' I was very aware that it was not the Psychic Medium's job to give me the answers I needed. They can only communicate the information they get from the spirit world in the way they receive it. They can spark something within us to trust and follow our intuition; ultimately, all the answers we need are within each one of us. Looking back, I think my intuition and faith were always leading me in the right direction. It was my lack of trust in my inner knowing that had me reaching out to others for the desperate answers I needed. The mediums I went to played a role in evoking a knowing and determination within me that we would find David and bring him home.

The desperation in me was willing to try anything that led us one step closer to finding David. I became fascinated at how we could connect with our passed on loved ones in spirit. I started to believe we were so much more intricately connected to our loved ones in spirit than we ever imagined.

I had also been gifted my very own pack of angel cards. I started to use these daily as another means to connect with David and get the guidance I needed. These brought me great comfort and support, especially when I needed it most in a world where I felt so lost, alone, and afraid. I got great solace in knowing I could call on my angels as well as David for added support. Instead of feeling like I was gaining more information at times, I felt like I remembered something I always knew. An inner knowing that I always had angels around me, protecting and guiding me. The difference now being, I was actively calling on them for help.

If someone asked me before my life took this turn what spirituality was, I am not sure what I would have answered. I would have thought it was all that 'hippie' stuff. It most definitely was not on my radar, that was one thing I knew. Now, I needed a belief in something, anything to make sense of everything that was going on in my life. I needed to believe I was part of something bigger than myself, a part of something that I did not understand but hoped one day I would get a greater insight into.I was aware that spirituality was becoming a part of my everyday life. I was willing and open to explore it on a deeper level. David was sending me signs in the form of animals and even people. I was receptive to all these signs; I longed for more to keep empowering and pushing me on. I believed he could see how the signs stirred something in me. They gave me hope and faith in the unknown. I made sure I shared this hope I had with everyone else. If David's girlfriend had hope we would find David, this would trickle down to everyone else.

A Special Person Sends A Special Person

This is the most important part of the book. This is where the veil began to thin between the world David was in and the world I was living in. This is where David showed he is always there and is a lot closer than I ever, in my wildest dreams, could have imagined. This is where he showed he would go to any lengths to guide and encourage me and that in this lifetime our relationship knew no boundaries, that love was stronger than anything else and that love could overcome all the odds that were against us. Looking back, David had been preparing me and guiding me up to this moment.

It was a Saturday evening; one I will never forget. At this stage, days meant nothing to me, but this day was different and so symbolic. I was more upbeat than I usually was. I had been to a medium earlier that day. I had been told we were going to find David and this was like music to my ears. They were the only words I ever needed to hear. Someone called to visit, and asked me how I was. I told them with pride that, "We were going to find David".

I then started telling the person about my angel cards and how I felt they gave me comfort. As she listened to me, I could tell she seemed preoccupied. Out of nowhere, she told me she had to tell me something. I did not overthink it. In the previous months, I had got good at listening to people but, really, I was not listening at all. There was sound with no volume. My head was in a different place, probably at the lake. I had mastered looking attentive and appearing interested, whilst being thousands of miles away.

She quickly got my attention and my ears pricked up when I was told that she had been seeing David over the last few months.

I sat up straight, and I think I stared at her continuously with utter dismay on my face.

It took a while for the words to come out. I think I said something like "That's not funny". My initial reaction was that she was making it up. As she looked at me, all I could see was emotion in her eyes. I trusted this person; she had no reason to lie to me. For a second, I thought maybe she was having some sort of mental breakdown. Over the last few months, she had shown extreme empathy and kindness towards me, whilst never trying to 'fix' me. She was always just there. I knew somehow that a deeper understanding of how I was feeling and what was going on for me existed. I looked into her eyes, and in that moment, something told me she was telling the truth. I did not know what was going on, but I was intrigued. My heart told me just to see how this was going to unfold.

I had been to mediums; I knew they connected with spirit. I had proof of it. I had faith and believed in their unique skills and abilities. They had told me things no one would have ever known. This was different because I knew this person. Often, before going to a medium, I would have been so nervous I would not have slept the night before. A few hours before I noted I even got a twitch in my leg. It was like my leg started doing an Elvis dance. I was not sure what the twitch was at the time. Since becoming familiar with energy, I think it was energy or spirit trying to give me another sign. On this night, I was caught off guard. I was not prepared for this. I was utterly shocked and lost for words. She then went out to her car and brought in a pack of angel cards and told me she had them for years. It was not hard to believe as these cards were battered, and all worn around the edges. One card even had a hole in it.

I started to feel so sorry for her. You could tell she was petrified; fearful I would not believe her; afraid I might tell someone. She was really going out on a limb telling me. My intuition never led me to think that she might not be telling the truth. I always believed. Again, here was David testing my faith and belief in the unknown. My belief and faith were strong; he was making sure of that. I knew he would have tried anything to try and connect with me.

You can imagine how the questions flowed out of me. I asked, "What do you mean, you see David?" I needed answers. This person went on to tell me that she sees David, connects with him and he gives her messages. I remember being flabbergasted thinking 'what on earth was going on?'

You could tell she was incredibly nervous; not knowing how I was going to take it. I offered her reassurance, I trusted her. I was honest and said I was a bit shocked and that I did not know how to react. I did not fully understand, and it was hard to get my head around it, but I knew I believed.

Out of nowhere, I asked, "Can you see David right now?" She replied "Yes", and even pointed out that David was standing right behind, me, minding me.

I watched her eyes gaze in the direction behind me, fixating on one spot. Tears plummeted down my face; it was so surreal. I asked a lot of questions; and she proceeded to describe what he looked like and what he was wearing, describing his mannerisms. It was him. It was strange because I knew David was always with me. To have someone you trust point him out in a room was so emotional. It was heart-warming but also so distressing all in one. I felt comfortable because he was there with me. But it was also so heartbreaking because I wanted to see David in the way she could see him. I cried at that moment as all I wanted was for him to put his arms around me and embrace me.

It felt so weird but so right, that is the closest way I can describe that night to. That night sparked a whole new journey between that person and I. Whether we liked it or not, we had been bonded together by David. Going back to my quote 'everything happens for a reason', there had to be a reason for this. I knew there was. I also knew the way my life was unfolding at some stage I was going to find out.

All I knew was this was just the start of something. David was as good as shouting from the rooftops 'I am here with you'. Little did I know what lengths he would go to. She left the house that night, and I went to bed. As I lay in bed that night, something was different. I did not want my mind to switch off like I usually would have. Instead, I wanted to analyse what was going on. Of all the things that could have happened, this was not something I could have ever imagined. I had been granted my very own personal medium. Someone I knew, loved and trusted. I knew David was with me always, but this was, again, confirmation of it.

94

This brought me great comfort but also a level of anxiety. What was going to happen next? Were there going to be other messages or was David going to go again just like the last time? I cried into my pillow like I usually did but, on this night, I had a little more comfort within my heart. Night-time, more than any other time, always seemed the loneliest. I knew one thing; this did not scare me. Alright, I did not understand it fully, but I was not afraid. I sat and pondered for ages; my mind was so active it even fought against the sleeping tablets. Why this person? Why now? What next?

Waking up, I remember jotting my head out of bed. Straight away I remembered last night. It was weird not waking up to the usual dread that was my life. Instead, I just felt confused, I kind of wondered had I dreamt last night. I lay in bed that morning for ages pondering my life and how it got to this. David's body was still missing in Canada presumed to be still in the lake. I say this because all we could be was hopeful. We really did not know what conditions the lake had thrown up since we had left in September. Did this mean David was going to tell us where he was? What was going on?

I would usually have stayed in bed to avoid making the day longer, but that day I got up. There was so much I needed to process. There was so much going on. My head was going around and around. This was the closest thing to David that I had now. I was going to embrace it with open arms. I wanted to call this person and get more information. I knew I had to let her come to me in her own time. This was a little bit frustrating; I just had to be patient. I was starting to learn; it was just easier to go with whatever life throws at you.

Eventually, I got hold of that wonderful person who we are going to call 'Sophie'. She has a fantastic gift, but for now, she is not ready to be recognised for her abilities and I will honour that for her.

I am sure she felt like she was on an episode of 'The Chase' because I kept firing questions at her and I could hear her anxiety. I thought maybe she regretted telling me. She told me she did not know why she decided to tell me last night, but that the urge came to her, and she just went with it and trusted her intuition.

Sophie informed me that she has been seeing David since his accident back in June and that she visually 'sees' David every day. While talking to me, she told me David was with me now - as he always was. Every time I heard this, I felt an intense pain around my heart and all I could do was cry. I asked why she did not tell me sooner? She said she had no intention of telling me at all and was equally surprised. She just got a feeling that night that the time was right. Later, in my spiritual journey, I discovered that this was her intuition. She had got a feeling, an urge from her soul instead of fighting it and going with her logical mind, she went with her instinct and her inner knowing.

We all have an intuition, but sometimes we get so caught up in the physical world we do what we think is sought of us, we listen to our head instead of our heart and inner voice. When these inner nudges come up, we resist them and put them to the back of our mind. I was so glad Sophie went with her intuition and told me. Sophie went on to tell me that she could see I was open and receptive to this information and that David had been preparing me for this moment. I felt this and believed this too.

She proceeded to tell me nobody else knew she had this special gift, not even her closest family. Sophie had gone out on a limb telling me and I respected her for that. I knew it was hard on her especially seeing all the emotions this brought up for me. My heart was still so broken and longed for David, but I was so glad she told me, every time she could see David it hurt because I wanted and needed to see him too. She went on to tell me that she had this gift for a few years and had tried to fight it and would rather not have it. She divulged that it was different when David started coming to her, she could not resist it. He was there, and he was not going anywhere anytime soon. It was so bittersweet. She disclosed to me that she had written down messages from David and that at the right time, they would be given to me.

To make things even more surreal, Sophie then told me she could also feel my energy. Now, back then, I did not have a clue what this meant. She went into depth and said that when she was in my presence, she could physically take on how I felt. She got emotional at this and told me it breaks her and David's heart to feel how broken I feel. Hearing this was so strange, and I felt sorry for her feeling how I felt. Nobody deserved to have to take those feelings on.

After chatting with her for a while, I could see why David had picked this person. She was so kind and gentle with a special air about her. There was no logic to this, just a feeling that I had to explore it.

Getting My First Message

Looking at the piece of paper with my first written message from David was heartbreaking and beautiful. I remember holding it with everything I had knowing deep in my heart that it was from David. My life was turning into a scene from 'PS I Love You' except this was not a film. This was my life. In the first note I received David recalled a memory from years ago. A memory Sophie could not have known about. I knew it was David. He was communicating to me through this person, it was so surreal. It felt like I had my very own earth angel.

She was able to bridge the gap between David and I. The gap that for so long I felt was getting drastically bigger was now starting to shorten. She provided me with the communication I was longing for from David. I would have done anything to have him back in the physical sense, but that was not going to happen, this was the next best thing.

I knew the type of relationship I had with David. It is hard to explain the special bond you had with someone and even more complicated when this relationship in the physical sense is gone. Sophie understood and could describe the beautiful relationship David and I had.

A beautiful relationship sparked from then on between Sophie and I. She became that person I called or texted for no apparent reason. On most days it was to ask "Is David there? Will you ask him if we are going to find him?" Sophie had the patience of a saint because I had her heart broken. Through her, David was sending me messages to uplift and inspire me. Some days these notes were the only thing that got me through the day.

At times, I thought Sophie started to know me better than I knew myself. Sophie would be liable to call me at any time during the day. I would receive phone calls saying "You're bad, aren't you?" I could hear the concern in her voice when she proceeded to tell me that David had told her to call me. She would say things like "David was worried". In the beginning, this shocked me. My faith was strong, and I knew he was always with me, even if at times I could not feel it, this proved he was with me. When I was struggling, somehow Sophie would know just when to phone me. David was right. I did need to speak to her. I needed to know he was there. I needed to hear that he loved me. I needed someone to tell me somehow everything was going to be ok. I needed to feel that he was close even though he felt a thousand miles away.

One day, I recall being at the side of the road in the car. I was so overwhelmed; my eyes were blurry I had been crying so much. I had to pull in as it was getting dangerous and I couldn't see the road in front of me. A part of me wanted to keep driving, I did not care what happened. Something stronger in me knew the right thing to do was to pull in, which I did. I was so fed up. Sophie rang me and could tell me exactly what had just happened and how I was feeling. In detail, she could describe my exact emotions. That day, she gave me that little bit of strength and encouragement to hold my head up no matter how heavy it felt. She understood, she got it.

Sophie was always so empathetic; even during the times I was so distressed and angry. I would plead with her that 'I didn't want to be here anymore', I would beg her to ask David, or whoever was up there, to take me too. I knew this was extremely hard on her. I also had a knowing I could be honest with her and tell her exactly how I was feeling.

Taking the Good Days with The Bad

On my 'good days', this newfound revelation was a blessing. On my 'not so good' days, I resented Sophie's gift. I couldn't understand why she could see David and I just had to just believe this was all real.

I started to research Google for some added support and guidance. David was a firm believer in Google solving all of life's problems; anything was worth a shot. It turns out, in fact, this is a common thing. A passed on loved one, will try and connect with you through any means possible. They would never want to frighten you or cause you further distress. They will only do this if you are receptive to this type of communication. They will find someone close to you and channel through them.

Sophie and I began to have this unbreakable special bond. We were bonded by something so surreal, nothing in this physical world could break it because we were connected by spirit. We were bonded by David. I needed more answers from David, though. The only question that I ever needed answered was, 'Were we going to find him?' It was so frustrating, but he was not giving me an insight into this at all. Nothing. He gave me lots of messages but would never delve into that. David's focus was to show me he was with me always and to develop my faith. This should have been enough and I can see that now but, at the time, it was not enough. I needed to know if we were going to find him.

The Lead up to Christmas

Christmas is supposed to be a happy occasion, a time to spend with the people who you love and care about the most. The lead up to Christmas kept highlighting the fact that David was no longer here. My family, and David's family all went to Tenerife for the holiday period just to get away for a while. There was strength and comfort in us all being together. We, too, had a bond that would forever be unbroken - bonded by pain, trauma and grief. More importantly, we were bonded over an infectious and undying love we had and would continue to have for David.

Even though Christmas was difficult, it meant we were one step closer to moving into 2018. Every year is supposed to be monumental, significant, whatever you want to call it. This year though all I wanted was one thing, I just wanted to find David. Well, I also wanted my life to go back to normal and to feel somewhat human again. I was willing to settle for finding him. Anything after that, I would deal with when the time approached.

We received pictures of the lake and it shocked me how the landscape looked so completely different. It was not the lake we knew, not the lake we left last September. The lake was completely covered with a thick sheet of ice. It was just so hard to believe David could have been under that big sheet of ice. That's what we were praying for anyway.

I was still receiving notes from David. I could not help but feel so lonely and sad, thinking of him somewhere all alone under that big sheet of ice across the other side of the world. That opened different scenarios in my mind's eye. What if David's body had moved? What would we do then? The thought of this scared me, but still it could have been a possibility. Nothing in this world led anyone to believe we would be any step closer this year to finding David.

My intuition and faith remained optimistic and nobody was going to take that from me. I had my own little David communicating with me - often daily. He was guiding me on and giving me the motivation I needed. I had a fire lit within me again. I had a purpose and a passion for succeeding in this mission of finding him.

Getting Our Focus Back

Approaching February and springtime, the momentum started moving. We were looking into flights and making plans to return to Kinbasket Lake. This time, we were going to find David and I did not care if anyone thought I was delusional or naïve believing this. David was clever and had prepped me the last few months with all the synchronicities and signs he had sent. I felt like I had an inner knowing; I did not need logic to back this up. I had a knowing that David was going to guide us to him, and we would bring him home.

I spent my days fantasising and imagining what that moment would look like. I think in my head I glamourised this moment and was a little bit unaware of the harsh reality of what finding David would look like. Getting closer to us returning to the lake, he slowly started giving us little clues about what the search may look like when we returned.

I would consistently ask Sophie, "Are we going to find David?" The message David repeatedly portrayed to me was, this was not important. It was more important to David that I felt him around me and gained the understanding and faith that he never left and that in one way through this new revelation I had already found him. I needed closure, though, I needed to find his physical body. I needed it for my mental health, to be able to process that this really had all happened. We all needed it.

Preparing for A Funeral

A few weeks before heading back to the lake, I went out and bought an outfit for David's funeral. When I bought it, I fully envisioned myself wearing it at his funeral. Throughout this journey, I have always been open and voiced what was going on in my head. I arrived home, showed my family the outfit and announced "This is what I will wear at David's funeral". Nobody directly said anything. They didn't need to. I could sense their concern and anxiety around this. Nobody seemed to be as optimistic as me, to a point I think people viewed my optimism as a default. I knew everyone wanted the same results as I did, of course, they did. I knew that my family and friends were afraid of the aftermath of what not finding David would look like for me. It was so apparent that it was the only thing holding me together. They had already seen the lows I had fallen to. They were being logical and taking in all the other factors that played a part in us finding David. It was a blessing in disguise that I was not one bit logical. David and I used to joke about this; we were opposites, he needed facts and figures but not me. I made my decisions more from an emotional place or a feeling I had. Reflecting even into my early teenage days, I think I was always like this. I used to joke with my friends in school, and one of my common phrases was 'I feel it in my waters'.

I would just get this feeling about an event or situation; maybe I was always in touch with my intuition unknown to myself. David and I had a good set up. Between 'my waters' and his logistics, we balanced each other out. 'My waters' this time were leading me to the belief that we would be successful in our endeavours. David would have been proud because we had a plan.

When Being Strong is the Only Option

I could not have been any more ready to return to the lake. My purpose was back; my reason for living. I was so focused on this I often could push the grief into the background, even if only for a short while. David was also giving me little messages about what the search may look like this time around. At times, I longed to tell people about my newfound connection with David. I remember one day being at a meeting with a dive team who were due to fly out to Canada to offer their expertise and professional support. As I was introduced to one the members of the dive team, his name rang a bell in my head. While shaking his hand, I remembered a message David had recently given me with this man's name in it. He told me that this man would be significant in the search this time around. My heart skipped a beat to the point I told this man a medium told me he was going to come and help us. I could not contain myself; David was finally helping guide us on the search.

On a few occasions, I was encouraged to plan for the scenario that we might not find David. I found this quite offensive, and I would not hear of it. I was not naïve but deep down, I was petrified. I knew all the odds were against us. I was scared of what would greet us and had crippling anxiety around this. The difference was my faith and belief outweighed all these emotions.

We were all, quite literally, praying for a funeral. We needed this closure for all this to sink in and feel real. Often, I used to trick my brain and tell myself David was working away, that he was not dead at all. I had the perfect scenario in my head. I had moved over to Ireland to live there for a short period. At times, I convinced myself that this could have been believable. We hadn't one bit of evidence to prove David was dead. Nothing. Sometimes I think my brain believed this. I sometimes wondered, had my mind fully processed that David was never coming back.

Tragedy Strikes Twice

It was exactly one week before we were due to go back to Canada when tragedy struck twice. I was pottering around upstairs, lost in my thoughts which was not unusual. In my head I had left Ireland, every day that passed was a day closer to getting back to the lake. All I thought about was David and the lake. I was consumed by the thoughts of it. I needed to be there.

It was a Monday afternoon; I cannot remember what I was doing; one thing I knew for sure was that I was not expecting visitors. You can imagine my surprise to hear my two friends in the kitchen downstairs. My first thought was 'oh no, visitors'. At times, I had convinced myself I was so busy that I could not entertain visitors, not that I was entertaining to be around anyway. To be honest, it was a full-time job, processing all the irrational thoughts that would come through my head.

It was very unusual for someone to call to the house without texting. I presumed I arranged the visit and forgot about it. I dragged myself down the stairs and put my brave face on. I put it down to grief brain that I forgot they were coming. Grief had a way of making your brain go to mush. In a way, I had nearly got used to it, so I did not pass any heed. At times I felt like the lights were on, but nobody was home, I was utterly absorbed in my little bubble.

I greeted my friends in the kitchen, and we all sat down at the kitchen table and starting chatting. I was so consumed by my thoughts. I did not even notice the look on their faces or sense that something was very wrong. I just thought they were checking in with me to make sure I was ok.

The conversation took a turn for the worst when they told me one of our close friend's boyfriend had tragically died. I do not remember what they said or how they said it; all I remember was the complete shock and distraught look on their faces. We all blankly stared at each other as we tried to process the terrible news we had just received. I thought there is no way this could be true; there was no way the world could be this cruel. I already felt like I was going crazy and I wondered was I having a nightmare from the sleeping tablets I had been taking.

After a few minutes, it became real as we were all still sitting at my kitchen table, looking at each other with no words. I did not know what to say and they did not know what to say. We all just cried at the devastating news. The shock was overwhelming thinking of what our poor friend was going through. We all cried thinking of her, and then cried some more. Her life had just been torn apart. I felt utterly numb to the core. I could not stop thinking of my friend and what she was going through right now. The thought of it made me start to feel physically sick. The fact that I had a slight idea of the pain that was sprung upon her made the feeling even worse.

It brought me straight back to when I heard about David. My heart broke for her, and I started to feel so angry. Why did this happen? Why would someone else have to go through this pain? I could not understand why this tragedy had happened to another young man; another family torn apart by such a tragedy. I felt so angry; I already thought the world was a cruel place taking my David, and on that day, the world appeared even colder and darker than I ever imagined. My mind went into overdrive. Why would anyone want to be a part of this cruel world? Like why? What was the point? I kept thinking about my friend, and it was so awful to know what she was going through. That hurt my heart even more.

I stayed with my friends for the evening and there was some comfort in us being together. We were all still together when my phone rang. It was my friend. I was so nervous about answering the call. I didn't know quite what to say to her, yet all I wanted to do was talk to her. You could tell she was heartbroken over the phone and I longed to take some of her pain away. Through the tears, I sensed she longed for me to give her reassurance. To tell her everything would be alright, to provide her with anything to try and make this nightmare easier. Her life had just fallen apart. I cried, and she cried, tears of pain. The thing was, I did not have any magic word to make any of this better or words to ease even an ounce of her pain.

I had to show her that somehow, we could do this. In that moment I did not know how or what that meant, but I made a promise to myself that I would do anything I could to help her. I had to be strong and be a guiding light for her, even if I felt like my light was burned out. I prayed to David to give her some inner strength and help look after her. I prayed to him to provide me with inner strength and guidance.

When I thought about the bigger scale of things, it made me so angry. Our situations were so similar.

Both of us were in long-term relationships, both in our mid-twenties. We had our lives planned with two men we loved and adored and just like that they were gone and life as we knew it was over. No warning signs, no anything. Just gone.

That week went by like a blur. I tried my best to support my friend. I did all I knew I could do, and that was to be there for her. I had so many conversations that week with David in my head. I could not understand why we were sent so much tragedy. In my grief journey that week, I carried the most anger. I held so much anger towards David; I often wondered could he not have prevented this, no one else needed to go through this pain. My anger was so conflicting because, on the other side, I missed him so much. I longed for him to be there to comfort me. I needed him. It was even more apparent that he was gone.

Often, that week I hugged my friend and it was a different kind of hug, a hug that bonded two broken women together. A hug that did not need words. That week, words served no purpose; they could not make anything better. A hug that held her and said I feel your pain because I too, was broken; a hug that felt sad, lonely and afraid.

A hug that also said I do not know or have the words to tell you this will be ok, but I have got your back. That week, all I could do was be there for my friend.

The day before I was due to go back to Canada, I met up with my friend who lost her partner and my other two friends, who are all graced with the most beautiful souls. We had met in college in Letterkenny a few years previous. We bonded straight away as we were all from Mayo. Little did we know in college that, years later, we would be connected further into our friendship by a double tragedy. Out of the four of us, two of us had lost our partners to bereavement. Our other two friends are walking angels, no doubt about it. For so long, they had been tasked with holding me together, and they would now do the same for this friend. They had been through so much pain and were heartbroken too, but they did everything and then some more to help support us both.

The four of us were all so broken, yet so strong, brave, courageous and loyal. We all hugged and prayed that after all the tragedy we had been through hopefully we would find David. One thing was certain within all the tragedy we all needed some good news.

Returning to The Lake for The Third Time

I felt shattered and broken, heading on the bus to Dublin airport. I was so focused on finding David, but now I could not help but think of my friend in Ireland and what she was going through. Indeed, David had to pull some strings up there. Had we all not been through enough? In my head, I pleaded with him. Enough was enough. We were not leaving Canada again without him. At times throughout the journey, a peaceful wave would wash over me. A feeling that even though everything was chaotic at the same time, everything was exactly as it should be. This time heading back to Canada with me, were David's parents, my sister and my Dad. We were one big family. We offered strength, guidance, support and sometimes even just a hug. We were a team.

I was surprised the airport did not know us on first name terms. In my eyes, the airport had turned from being an exciting place, a place where you embark on an exciting adventure to a place of dreaded fear. I just needed to get to the other side as quick as possible.

Landing into Calgary and feeling the Canadian air hit my face, it all started to feel real. Seven months later, we were back to finish what we started. We had a reason to be alive again. We had a focus, a mission. We were going to find David and make him so proud. I consistently spoke to David in my head. I promised him if we found him, I would get on with my life afterwards. I kept envisioning his funeral. In my head, I knew exactly what it would look like. I even had a list of songs that I had picked out.

Things started moving quickly when we arrived in Golden where we would be staying. We had lots of organising to do so we were kept busy. Our minds were so focused; we did not have time to dwell on what was going on.

It was our third time returning to the lake to search for David. As the saying goes, 'third time lucky' and hopefully this would be the case for us.

I felt like I was on the right soil. This time, like the others, no stone would be left unturned. We were focused, determined and we were going to find David and bring him home.

Our First Day at The Lake

Arriving back at the lake was never going to be easy and we were under no illusions of that. It's hard not to go back to that memory of what the lake took from us, making the instant connection that this was the place that stole our David. A place that turned our whole world upside down in what felt like a microsecond.

This time, it was like arriving at a different place. The landscape and scenery were not familiar; it was not the place we last left. I think this was a good thing like David had planned it as it was not as startling to the system. It was a strange feeling and felt like we had all been transported somewhere else. Everything was so different, even the weather. We were used to warm weather even, at times, being blistering hot. On that day, it was cold and brisk; we were surrounded by snow and ice, tons of it everywhere. It was all so hard to comprehend. It was also so quaint around the lake with the campsite still being closed; it was so unfamiliar to have no one else at the lake. My mind could not help but think maybe this was another thing David had planned. The first thing we all seemed compelled to do was walk towards the bridge. A place we spent weeks last summer staring out onto, praying that we would find him. As we looked out onto the lake, it was covered with a clean sheet of ice. It was so hard to imagine that somewhere under that ice was our David. The dock did not even seem to exist with all the snow and ice.

The first job on our list was to clear a path down to the lake. We were all eager and got straight to work. Shovels in tow, we started to make a path. I think we can all agree that shovelling snow is not the most enticing job in the world. On that day, I held that shovel with pride; I had never been so happy to use a shovel. To me, it meant so much more than shovelling snow. We were progressing; we were one step forward, one step closer. If there were a prize for my attempt, I would have won it. It was cold and hard work, but none of that mattered.

I was determined, focused, and rearing to go. I felt like the proudest person in the whole world. Gratitude exuberated from me. I was going to put my all and then some more into finding David.

The Closest I Ever Felt to David

After we had made our path, we all got to walk down and stand out on the lake. It was so surreal standing on the lake; my two feet touching the ice where typically the water lay. We did not know the lake in this form. We only knew the lake from spending so much time out on it in boats. This took 'different' to a whole new level. My mind was racing. I thought this possibly could be the closest I have ever been to David. Then, some irrational thoughts started to play in my head. It was a good thing I had to somewhat focus on not falling on the ice.

We spent a few hours walking around the lake and searching, staring at the ice with nobody saying too much. I think we were all a little bit lost for words. As I stared at the ice, I felt petrified at the thought of finding something that may be of significance. What would it look like? What would I do? I felt so grateful to know that in the next few days we had professionals coming to help us search for David. As I looked around, it became clear we were out of our league here with the condition the lake was in.

This search was completely different from the last one. In the early days, it was mostly done on foot on the ice and the land. As the days progressed and the water began to melt, the channels began to get exposed. This meant we could just about get a boat into the water. And when I say just about, I do mean just about. This was a significant advancement, as it meant we could get the canine search and rescue team out into the water. They had previously assisted us in the last search and were due to arrive in the next few days.

The First Few Days

Once the ice started to melt, we were all so aware this was our window of opportunity. We had a short period; we needed to make sure we had every resource possible to make sure this search was successful. I had another tool in my toolbox. I had David. He continued to send motivating messages to encourage us and push us on.

It sounded simple we just needed to find David. Once we did, I knew that I would have to embark on another journey. I would somehow have to try and make peace with all that had happened. I hoped and wished that somehow, one day, this might all make a little more sense to me.

The more days I spent at the lake, the more my head thought about my life, my future. I was so focused, yet I was constantly fretting over what could happen next. Deep in my soul, I knew I could not use finding David as a 'get-out' clause to life forever. For now, it was acceptable because I was angry and I was very resistant to accepting that any of this was ok. My mind was working in peculiar ways; here I was at the lake thinking about the next step my life may take. I think it was starting to hit me what we would be dealing with when we did find David. I could not help it, but every time I looked at the ice, I thought of a scene from the 'Walking Dead'. Ironically, this was a programme David and I became fascinated with over a few series.

The biggest question my head was trying to process was what was he going to look like when we found him?

For the last few months in my bubble, I had this image in my head of finding David as he was. The David

I kissed and said goodbye to the morning he headed off to the tournament. The only difference being this time his eyes would be shut forever. I imagined being able to see his face and being able to touch his soft, delicate skin. He really did have the smoothest skin; I would have done anything to have felt it one last time. To lay a kiss on his forehead, to tell him it's ok if he really must go.

As I stared at the ice, it was clear my mind had created the most unrealistic account of what was going to happen. Deep down this was wishful thinking I knew exactly what we were dealing with. I just still wanted to find him alive and well. Our minds have a way of keeping us safe and protected and mine was willing to create any scenario to do this.

Against All the Odds Finding David

We had now been at the lake for a few days with no success in our efforts. On this morning, we were all eager to arrive at the lake. We had the canine search team arriving. They were terrific at what they did; we were all in awe of their professional abilities. My heart felt so grateful to have them helping us again. When we landed at the lake, we greeted them with open arms and lots of hugs. You could feel their energy; they were eager to get moving and get onto the lake.

They had to get set up and it took a while for things to get moving. There was not much for us to do but watch on. It was a little bit frustrating and my anxiety felt like it could have peaked at any minute. Often, five minutes felt like an hour and your eyes would get sore from staring out at the lake. At the same time, you would be terrified in case you might miss something important.

It was the waiting around and the eagerly anticipating that I found the hardest. It's bizarre really; I was often so far removed from what was going on I could disassociate from the fact we were looking for David's body. Then, in another moment, it would hit me. I would stare at the lake and all I could do was cry. I had to. I had to let some of the intense emotions out. I had got so used to crying if it wanted to come, I would just let it out. When I started crying, it was not pretty. To me, it felt like a beast had taken over my body. I was very aware it was quite traumatic to watch. It felt like my whole body would go into panic mode. It was so overwhelming; I did not know how to cope, so I just cried.

The new puppy recruits that the search team brought were a great distraction. They were so tiny and cute. When asked to look after one of them, I jumped at the job. It gave my mind a distraction. I remember looking at that puppy thinking how amazing is it that they will soon be trained to help people like me find their loved ones? In my eyes, dogs are the most amazing animals; they show you love unconditionally, especially when you need it most.

In the afternoon, all our anxieties were high. You could feel everyone's frustrations. We all just wanted anything that we felt would lead us one step closer to finding him. I longed to get the results needed, everyone did. I could not even dare to say how against the odds we were, in my eyes that was an extremely negative way of looking at our situation.

I continued to stare out onto the lake. Watching the dogs, my heart yearning for them to bark or give us a glimmer of hope. Every time I checked my phone, I kept seeing the numbers 2 and 222. I did not think much of it in the beginning. After a few hours of repeatedly seeing it, I said it to my sister; she agreed it must have meant something. This gave me the boost and hope I needed. I knew David was with us as always, and this was a sign. He was good at giving me a glimmer of hope exactly when I needed it, and I needed it on that day.

We decided to all go for a drive, needing to take a breather. The tensions were high, and we were all frustrated with the waiting around. In the car, nobody really said much. What was there to say? We did not need words; we just needed to find David. I started to think about how David was showing me the number 222. What did this mean? What was he trying to tell me? I tried to Google what it meant, but my phone would not work. I knew this was significant and I would check what it meant later.

Ironically, while driving back over the bridge that David had jumped off, my phone started to pick up coverage again. I attempted to put it into a Google search and just as I was about to read it, I could see two of the dog handlers walking towards the car. Something about this startled me, it was apparent they wanted to talk to us. We stopped the car and waited for them to approach us. We had been dealing with search teams for the last few months, so we did not think anything of it. We had grown accustomed to thinking we were going to receive the news we wanted and then we would hear something else. We just assumed they needed supplies, or something was wrong with the boat.

They walked up to the car window and made sure we could all see them. You could tell instantly that their interaction this time was different. We had grown a rapport with these people and you could just tell by their faces that they had found something. My heart started to beat as fast as it possibly ever did. I knew in that moment they had found him. They had found David.

I do not remember exactly how the words came out or what they said to me, that did not matter. Surprisingly, my first reaction was to get out of the car. I had been waiting so long for these words, yet I did not know what to do. My body wanted to collapse on the bridge, but I stood upright. I walked to the side of the bridge to the exact spot where David had jumped in. My legs proceeded to feel like jelly as I looked over the side of it. As I looked out, I could see the other dog handlers guarding what must have been David. All I could see was a sheet of plastic with a stone either side, which was obviously covering something. I could feel an overwhelming pressure in my chest and tears streamed down my face. I was terrified. I wanted to feel happy we had done it, but I was even more heartbroken, which I did not think could have even been a possibility. I had played this moment over and over in my head, yet I did not know how to react.

My legs wanted to run, but my feet froze. I just stared down at that sheet of plastic. For those few moments, I did not want anyone to come near me, to embrace me. I did not want to listen to anyone. I just wanted to be by myself. I was so overwhelmed I thought I had prepared for this moment, but it turns out I had not. People were talking, but I could not hear the words. I continued to stare out at the lake, trying to get my head around what was going on. We had found him yet why was I feeling like this? Why was I not happy? I knew I felt grateful, but I also felt so broken and shocked.

After a few minutes, we all embraced each other and discussed our next move. I knew I needed to get closer to that sheet of plastic which was covering something on the ice. We were all given the option of going down to the lake to identify David. Intuitively, I wanted to go down, but I knew that I would be advised against it. At this stage, I had been through so much I did not think this was going to be the deciding factor that was going to send me over the edge. When I want to be, I can be very stubborn. I was going, and nobody was going to stop me.

I knew I was strong enough for this and if not, David would send me some more inner strength. I needed to do this. It all happened so fast I needed to see for myself to believe it was real. I had watched videos of what bodies looked like when they are recovered. I had prepared as much as I could have for this moment.

It was only a few metres walk from the bridge down to the lake, but it felt like it took an eternity. I cried most the way down wondering how my body was even carrying me down there. I felt empty but full of energy. It must have been all the adrenaline rushing through me.

As I got closer and closer to the lake, my heartbeat was pounding out of my chest. I had never experienced feelings like this before. I thought with everything I had gone through so far; the feelings could not have become any more intense.
I was defying my own beliefs because these feelings were very new to me and even more amplified and overwhelming.

As we got closer, you could see one of the dog handlers cry as we approached him. He hugged me so tight; he was as emotional as us all. I thanked him for what he and his team had done for us. You could tell his heart was broken for us, but also at the same time the relief he felt for us.

I remember touching the plastic sheet thinking somehow David was under there. In that moment, it felt like I had just found out David had died; my body just went into shock mode. I think I let out a scream, but to be quite honest, I do not remember. Then, they lifted the sheet of plastic so we could identify David. It was a very informal identification; we were under no illusions it may take days or even weeks for this to be formally done. I do not think I knew what I was going to see, but I was not expecting that. It did not look like David, not the David I wanted it to look like anyway. It resembled a body, which freaked me out. I knew, at that moment, it had to be David. Under that sheet of plastic lay David. His body briefly exposed from under the ice. The intensity of what I was feeling startled me. Was this even real? Was I dreaming?

I got a few minutes with David by myself sitting beside the piece of plastic on the ice and just crying. I kept rubbing my hand over the plastic sheet talking to David. I kept telling David I was there. I was with him. In that moment, I felt so distraught but also so appreciative to be able to do this. We had been granted a miracle. But now it was very apparent, David was gone.

As I sat with David, I told him I would somehow try and figure this all out. Somehow, I would try to navigate this new life, the one that was a far cry from what I wanted. The one that I still was so resistant towards and did not wish to navigate. For now, I had to let all this sink in. My mind drifted to the thought of David's body being stuck under the ice. I started to cry again; this was awful. The David I knew and loved was here, stuck under a sheet of ice. Tears dropped from my eyes as I clung to the sheet of plastic, I clung to the closest physical piece of David I was going to get. Why had this happened? Why was David gone? We had so much planned so much we needed to do. I needed him at that moment more than ever.

Once the initial shock settled and the reality that we had found David sunk in, I got an elated feeling. A feeling of accomplishment, we had done it we had found him. I missed him terribly and even more so on that traumatic day. Ringing home to tell my Mum was when it hit me that we had found him. A phone call I had rehearsed in my head many times over. I had spent the last few months longing to get those three words out of my mouth, "We found him, we found David".

I knew my Mum already knew, but I had to say it for myself, I needed to get those words out to make it all feel real. I could hear the emotion in my Mums voice as I said it "We found him". I don't think she could hear the words with all the emotions that came out with them. I had to repeat them a few times for her to understand what I was saying. To hear her reaction on the other side of the phone, the shock in her voice, the dismay, but the overall sigh of relief. Someone referred to the news as the 'happiest, saddest news they ever heard'. Two vastly different feelings, I exuberated gratitude for the miracle we had just received, but it also conflicted with the pain I felt as it was so immense.

The next few hours, we had to wait for the police and the coroner to arrive and assess the scene. With each professional service that came, the reality of what had just happened sank in. Even the professional services informed us they did not think we would be successful in our search for David.

After the scene was assessed, we were told by the police that as David's body was submerged under the ice, he was essentially stuck. That did not shock any of us, but we were then informed as a result of this we would have to wait for a specialist team to arrive in the morning. This specialist team would be qualified in recovering bodies from these conditions.

My first thought was we cannot leave him here overnight as we have just found him. I even asked could I stay there with him for the night. It was extremely hard, but we had no choice. We could not stay, and the specialist team would not arrive at the lake until the morning. We were offered lots of reassurance and encouragement that David would be fine overnight. A part of me could not help but think what if an animal got to his body during the night. A plan was made that a police officer would stay at the lake and watch David's body 24/7 until the morning. This put our minds at ease a bit.

Leaving the lake that evening was a different feeling; we did not have the frustrations we had on other days when we did not get the results we needed. On that evening, our hearts were full of pride and we were so grateful that we had found David. That night, we brought the Canine Search Team out for dinner to thank them. A dinner did not suffice for what they had just done for us. Words could never be expressed for what they had done for us. They had granted us something our hearts longed for and needed to receive. However hard and traumatic all this was, we were finally getting the closure we needed. For now, David would have wanted us to celebrate our accomplishment, to celebrate him and to celebrate miracles.

Guiding Us with Numbers and Signs

That evening, I thought back to the way I kept seeing the number 222 earlier that day. I previously did not get a chance to read what it meant so I searched it again. The first search page that came up read 'trust that everything is working out exactly as it is supposed to, with Divine blessings for everyone involved. Let go and have faith'. I was astonished in amidst all the fear and the anxiety David was trying to tell me everything was going to be ok. I then thought back to the previous night, when I had used my angel cards for some guidance and received the miracle card. After the day we had, I started to see a little bit of magic in the world around me. I knew he was guiding us. I had known for a long time. It was getting so much clearer now. He was trying to tell us all along that we were going to find him soon and we did.

That night I rang Sophie; she kept telling me how proud David was of us all. I told her that he was trying to tell me on that day we were going to find him. I was elated telling her this; she just said that she knew, she told me that 'David always has a plan'. Sophie could sense my anxiety about what was to come next, she kept offering me lots of reassurance and assured me David would be with me every step of the way in this new part of my journey.

I don't think I slept a wink trying to process what had happened but also trying to put together in my head what tomorrow may look like. I assumed he would be identified. We all knew it was David, of course, it had to be. We still needed confirmation of this to be 100%

sure. One thing was certain we were one big massive miracle step closer to bringing him home to Ireland.

Arriving Back at The Lake

It was so surreal waking up the next morning, our first time waking up after finding David. Nothing prepares you for the reality of it. My body and mind were exhausted, yet at the same time, I felt filled with so much energy. I remember sitting out on the porch that morning with a coffee in my hand. I felt afraid at what the morning entailed, of getting David out of the lake. I wondered what I would see. This is all we wanted, but this overwhelming sense of fear rushed over me.

There was little conversation in the car to the lake; we were filled with anxiety and fear of what lay ahead. I wondered would the specialist team be all kitted out in gear? I imagined so. I hoped that it was not very cold and that David would be treated with dignity and respect as they were retrieving his body.

When we arrived, it looked exactly like a scene from Crime Scene Investigates. Our initial reaction was to walk onto the bridge. We all watched on as the specialist forensic team removed David's body from the ice.

It was the universe's saving grace that it was so quiet at the lake. I am sure it was part of the plan. It was just us and a few of the locals we had grown close to watching on. The locals had taken us in and showed us kindness and compassion when we needed it most. It was so heartwarming and humbling to have them stand with us and support us. They never met or knew David, but they were as emotional as us and you could feel in their hearts, they were both happy and sad for us. It was ironic that we all stood on the bridge where

David's accident occurred. From a distance, we could see them trying to retrieve his body from the ice. I was glad we could only see from a distance; we could not see the smaller details of what this involved. We had also ended up arriving late.

At the time I was annoyed about this, but as I overlooked the lake, I could see that David was, once again, pulling strings, of all the moments throughout this journey, watching them retrieve David from the lake was the hardest.

My body ached, along with my mind and my soul watching this. I was so grateful, but the pain was immense. Although ten months had now passed, it felt like David had just gone. It now felt so real. I thought back to the counselling I had been attending, complicated grief was mentioned. There was no denying my life had got complicated. I was looking out onto the lake feeling as broken as ever and wondered had I just started grieving all over again? I self-diagnosed myself with complicated grief. I had prepared for this moment, but all the feelings were so devastating.

I knew that even at my worst, David would somehow send me the inner strength I needed. I already was so strong; there was no denying that. I kept reassuring myself at how far I had come. I could do this. I could do this for him. I would hold on with everything I had to bring him home.

Braving the Elements

It was dreadful being at the lake, witnessing David's body being retrieved. It all felt real when you could see a body bag laying on top of the ice. From a distance, the body bag looked long; there was no denying that there was a body in there, but not just any body. It was David's body. We could not hear anything, so we all muttered what we thought was going to happen next. We looked on as we watched the specialist team place the body bag onto a snowmobile. This was then used to escort his body up from the lake.

I instantly thought of David, the big adrenaline junkie he was. He would have often mentioned at some stage how he would have liked to experience a snowmobile. It felt warped to me that this was the how and the when. Another part of me for a second felt a little bit of comfort. I took it as a sign that David was up there planning all of this. Everything even down to getting an escort on a snowmobile.

The search to find David involved lots of new experiences and vast amounts of different equipment and technology. I felt like we had quite possibly seen it all, from a remotely operated underwater vehicle to top of the range sonar equipment. We had driven boats, spent more time in helicopters than you would even wish to imagine, we had come up close and personal to bears, we got the whole camping experience whether we wanted to or not, dealt with top of the range drones and the list could go on and on. Now, he could add the snowmobile onto his list of experiences. As we watched the snowmobile escort his body from the lake, we all instinctively walked over to meet David.

Getting Closer Than We Ever Imagined

We walked down from the bridge and were greeted by the Royal Canadian Mounted Police Service, the Coroner and the Forensic Team. They all sympathised with us, and it was touching to see the emotion on all their faces.

The coroner informed us David would have to be taken away to be formally identified. He told us he did not know how long this would take. I asked if we would see him when they had fixed him up? He just looked at me and replied, "No. You will not see David again". A little part of me was still clinging onto this, and in my head, I just wanted to see my beautiful David, even if only for a few seconds. I could not take my eyes off the body bag as we spoke; the reality of this was getting more apparent. That morning I had taken a Xanax tablet, and at that moment, I was extremely glad of it.

They let us say our goodbyes to him. This involved us each getting a few minutes with David and being able to place our hands on the body bag he was in. It sounds colder than it was. I put my hands on that bag, knowing David was there. I did not need him to be formally identified; we all knew it was him. The pain hurt so bad, but I also felt so thankful of this precious moment we had been granted. There was so much love within all the pain.

The next time we would see him would be in Dublin Airport when he would be in a coffin. All we could do until then was wait. I will not lie; I do not even remember what we did the rest of that day. I think we were all still in shock that we had found him.

All We Could Do Was Wait

We were at a standstill until David was formally identified. Looking back, it was a standstill we all needed. A time to breathe to try and take in everything that had happened. It helped that the weather had picked up; we all needed some vitamin D.

Over the next few days, I received many phone calls and texts from friends and family. They all had so much empathy for us, often saying how awful it must be for us all since we found David not being able to return to Ireland. I did not know how I felt but it was not awful. I needed this time. It felt strange and unfamiliar, but I felt peaceful. I could not put my finger on it, but something told me I was exactly where I needed to be.

Formally Identified and Getting a Little Piece of David

We all knew we had found David and the day he was formally identified just confirmed what we all knew to be true. This meant we could start organising how we would get him home. After he was formally identified, we had to go into the Coroner's office to meet him and discuss our plans. As we could not see his physical body, the Coroner agreed to get us some of his hair. I didn't even think this would have been a possibility, I just needed a little something in the physical sense to make sense of everything.

I never imagined I could possibly feel so many emotions holding strands of hair, not just anyone's hair, it was David's. Since moving to Canada, David's hair had gone quite grey. I often used to refer to him as a 'silver fox'. I laughed and cried delicately caressing the strands of hair in my hands. There was no denying it was David's hair, with some extra grey strands standing out.

Healing Times

We could now start planning and organising David's funeral. It felt like we were all in the calm before the storm. I was so apprehensive and afraid to go home even though we would be going home with him. Going home was different now. It was final. I was scared of what being at home looked like now we had found him.

We had now spent two weeks in Golden. My perspective on the place changed. I thought forever I would associate this place as the place that ruined my life. A part of me still believed that another part of me was aware it was an incredibly beautiful, peaceful place to be. It was like David was trying somehow in all the chaos to give us some happy and peaceful memories from a place that took so much away from us.

It was time to go home. Finally, we had put all the plans in place, we would fly on the same flight home as David and meet him in the mortuary in Dublin Airport. I do not think I could have felt any more afraid; everything was getting so real. I knew seeing and feeling his coffin, there would be no denying that he was gone.

It was time to say goodbye to the lake, this time on quite different terms. This time I could say it was our final goodbye—this time we had found David. The last few weeks I spent there I felt like I made some peace with the lake. On a beautiful sunny day, there is nowhere else you would rather be. The sun beating down on the majestic lake made it breathtaking.

Saying goodbye to the lake, it felt like I had to also say goodbye to another part of myself. I knew returning to Ireland with David meant in time I would have to try and navigate this new life that lay ahead of me. Then, and there, that looked unimaginable to me. Staring out onto the lake, I pleaded with him and whispered, 'please have a plan for me'.

Landing Back in Ireland and Meeting David

Arriving at Dublin Airport was a completely different experience to the previous times. During the flight home, I often felt like pinching myself; we had done it we had found him. This made me feel so proud and gave me such a sense of achievement. Other times, I cried because it hit me that he was gone for good. Two very conflicting emotions took over my mind and body, especially when we went to pick him up from the morgue to bring him to Mayo. The one thing I associated with someone who has died, is a coffin, as my hand rested over David's coffin reality sank in. We got ready and left the morgue; it was time to head home to Mayo.

My heart exuberated gratitude as we drove behind the hearse from Dublin to Mayo. Looking on from behind, I found it hard to take my eyes off his coffin. I felt so heartbroken but I tried to push this feeling down and focus on the fact we had found him. When we arrived outside David's house, the local community had gathered to greet us. The town was out in force, everyone just so relieved and happy that we had found him. It indeed, was something special with everyone coming together. David had not only bonded people, he had also bonded communities together.

David's Funeral

David's funeral was perfect, we had time to organise it and we had it planned to perfection. Often, when people die, the time between their passing and burial is very quick. One thing we had been granted was lots of time. Something I viewed for so long as a curse I was starting to see as a hidden blessing.

We had David waked in his home house for two nights. Seeing people's reactions when they arrived to sympathise with us was so heartwarming. You could feel the relief lift off people when they saw his coffin laid out. People needed to see it themselves to believe it to be true. People hugged us a little tighter than before, telling us they were 'so happy for us' often, then realising happy was not the most appropriate word and sometimes getting a little awkward. We understood, though, I do not think there is a word in the dictionary, to sum up, what we were all feeling. One thing was for sure though; everyone was so proud of us. The sheer strength and determination we showed to get to this moment, was something out of this world.

On the first night of David's wake, I slept on a blow-up bed beside his coffin. That night as I lay there staring at his coffin I cried. I missed him so much. I cried because I was sleeping beside his coffin. It was hard to process; he was in there. I realised I was afraid of everything else except death itself. I knew wherever David was, it was beautiful, and he was at peace. I could just feel it.

The hardest bit of the funeral I thought was putting David's coffin into the ground. How could that be easy? I think it is because it is the last bit of the funeral; everything else is just a lead up to this moment. Watching them put him into the ground, I felt my body shake. It was so overpowering, so final. I had to try and keep reminding myself that he was with me then and there. He was there always. David's soul was not being put into the ground. It was right beside me.

The weeks and months after his funeral were so difficult. In one way, the funeral was not the most challenging part, but it is when everything quietens down, that you are left with your thoughts. My mind now had the time to process the last few weeks, and everything that had just happened. The adrenaline of finding David began to wear off. My body was tired. I had been on overdrive for so long. It was time to give my body a break and just rest.

Our Healing Expedition

In August 2018, three months after we buried David, David's parents, his sister and I all headed back to Canada. We met with the Canine Search Team who had found David. We presented them with a donation. It meant so much to us to be able to give back and help other families who unfortunately would be in the same position we were in. To us, the donation was a small gesture for what they had done for us. In our eyes, we would never fully be able to repay them. They had granted us the biggest blessing, a miracle; they had given us closure, something which for so long seemed so far out of our reach. They were so emotional when we presented them with the donation; they too were aware of how this could help other families and the work they do.

They were going to use the money to buy a new boat to assist in the work they do. They told us they were going to put David's name on the side of the boat with a little dragonfly symbol. This made me feel so grateful as his legacy would live on and help so many others.

We spent two weeks in Canada, and again this journey offered us all some healing. It gave me lots of time to think and reflect. We had found David. I could not use that as an excuse anymore for avoiding life even if at all costs I still wanted to.

Making Little Changes

When I returned to Ireland, I knew I had to make some changes. Deep down, I knew I eventually would have to think about returning to work. I also had this knowing David was going to make sure this happened sooner rather than later.

My days consisted still of mostly sleeping, eating, walking the dogs and, of course, my daily dose of Dr. Phil. I had convinced myself that I could not return to work because I would miss my midday hit of Dr. Phil. I knew that was not true at all. I was terrified of change or anything outside of the routine I had created. My routine protected me from the outside world; it made me feel safe and secure. This, in turn, helped my anxiety. For so long, I felt so unsafe and so unsure, riddled with anxiety. It was just easier to stay cooped up in my safety net. To surround myself with the people I knew and loved, letting anyone else in scared me.

A part of me also felt that going back to work was such a normal thing to do. In my eyes that was unjust to David, it was like moving on. I felt so stuck because I knew I needed to try and push forward a little bit, yet I was heavily stuck on what had happened.

Through the messages I was receiving from David, he too, was telling me it was time to return to work. This caused me deep frustration as it was not just as easy as that, it meant facing my fears and anxieties. I knew if he was saying it, I must have been able for it.

Facing My Fears

Over the last year, I had been through so much trauma. I had witnessed and gone through so much. Yet applying for a job brought up a huge amount of fear and anxiety for me. Through lots of persuasion and encouragement, I applied and filled out an application for a job. I had little motivation or enthusiasm, but I still did it, and that was an achievement. One of the questions on the application form was to describe your proudest moment to date? I did not have to think twice and I put down that it was finding David and bringing him home.

It is probably not something you should put on an application form, but to me, it was the truth. I thought that it might also be a deterrent that they might think I was too traumatised and not ready to return to work. In one way that was what I thought, I was prepared to take half a step, not the full one yet. Someone, however, was ready for me to take the full step, and I remember being annoyed at getting called for an interview. I was annoyed at David; I saw it as him pushing me out of my comfort zone. Why was he not listening to me? I didn't feel ready.

The job involved working in the youth sector. I was barely able to support myself, never mind supporting other people. I had convinced myself at the interview they would realise how unstable I was, and there was no way I would get the job.

That was just wishful thinking and after the first interview, I was called for a second one. I quickly realised it was just easier to go along with it than fight against it. You could say I surrendered. At any stage, I could have decided not to go to the interview, but I didn't. I even prepared and enjoyed preparing for the second interview. Then it hit me even though I had decided that I did not want to be a part of any of this, here was David again pushing me on, trying to give me a purpose in life.

It is not hard to believe that I got the job and was forced back into normality with a big loud bang. Normality to everyone else but not to me, all the same I knew I just had to embrace it.

The anxiety of going from my small little circle and my routine was so terrifying, even more so than being at the lake searching for David. It brought me many sleepless nights before I started. I had this repeating thought that everyone would judge me, that I forever would be the woman who lost her partner in such a tragic way. I feared having a meltdown in the office in front of people; I feared the small chat, would I be able to handle it if someone was giving off about their significant other - something which I would have done anything to have been able to do.

David knew how much of a massive step this was for me. I continued to get notes from him pushing me on and he kept telling me this was all part of his plan. He had not led me astray yet, so I thought I had to do it no matter how afraid I felt.

I Am Trying to Find my Feet

The first two months were very tough being back at work. I came home nearly every evening crying and, in the mornings, I was riddled with anxiety going in. It was quite impressive the façade I had when I got to work. To the outer eye I appeared to be calm and have everything under control. But this was not the case.

Grief is often viewed in the physical sense and if you are not an emotional mess and crying to the visible world, then you must be ok. I did not feel one bit ok. My mind was in a constant loop trying to process my life and where it was heading. In work, I was calm, cool, collected, but a bag of anxiety on the inside. I was doing my best to fit in, but in my head, I felt like I stuck out like a sore thumb.

I felt bitter being back living at home and wondered should I move back to Vancouver. I was self-aware enough to realise that grief was going to follow me wherever I went. I just wondered when it was going to stop hurting so bad; I missed David so much.

The only positive was that it was a distraction. As I was working full time, by Friday I was wrecked, and fit for nothing. I would rest for the weekend and then on Monday do it all again. I was in survival mode - get up, go to work, go to bed, and then do it all again.

Christmas Comes Around Again

Eight months after finding David, Christmas flew in around the corner. Surprisingly, I was looking forward to having two weeks off work, with my main intention of sleeping. As regards the festivities, I was the equivalent to the Grinch. I did not care for Christmas, the decorations and everything else that came with it. Christmas was a time to spend with the people you love. The person I loved was not here and, in my eyes, Christmas was only highlighting that fact even more so.

This would be my second Christmas without David; I knew it was going to be hard, but I thought it would be a little bit easier than last year. It took a few days for me to realise how wrong I was. I found those two weeks excruciatingly painful. So painful I wondered did I feel anything last Christmas at all. It was like the walls came rushing in on top of me. I wondered was it because I was now off work, I had no distractions. I now had two weeks to sit with my feelings. Had I been bottling them all up? If I had, they were all seeping out.

I felt like I had not improved whatsoever in my life. I was my own most prominent critic. I used to dislike the saying 'time is a healer' but here I was judging myself. In my eyes, I had taken one step forward and twenty steps back. A part of me wished I felt better and that I could have embraced the festivities even just a little bit.

One day over the two weeks, I remember begging David to take me with him, I could not bear it here any longer. I remember lying on my bed, crying my eyes out. I had reached an all-time low. I knew I could not continue my life like this; I was only surviving; I was not living. I felt dreadful. I became aware that a little part of me wanted to be feeling better, a part I was not aware of before.

I was terrified of change; there was no denying that. One thing was starting to terrify me even more, and that was the thought of feeling this pain forever. I could not feel like this forever, could I? I was also losing my connection with David, even over Christmas, his messages struggled to motivate or uplift me. I needed something, anything to make everything less painful.

Part Two:
My Self-healing
Journey Began

I got so much healing from writing the first half of this book. I had to go back and revisit everything from the moment I heard about David's accident. I started writing this book in August 2019 and it's now fourteen months later. Even rewriting bits, I became aware of how much I have grown as a person.

Throughout this journey on my darkest of days, I often wished I could catch a glimpse of my future life. I just wanted to see if it would get any easier, anything to give me hope that somehow, I would make it out the other side of this horrible ordeal. Back when I was so consumed by my grief, I believed I was going to feel this overwhelming pain and grief forever. Anyone who is reading this who is struggling, I promise you 'it gets easier', words that for, so long, I never imagined would leave my mouth.

Throughout the bleakest of times in my life, I found an inner strength and resilience I never knew existed. I now know that David was guiding me through and pushing me on. I just had to have faith and believe that I was supported and that one day my life would get easier and more manageable. One thing David engrained in me on this journey was the importance of always remaining hopeful. Once you have hope, you have something to cling onto and guide you through even the most challenging situation.

I believe this is why my journey panned out exactly the way it did. Life had taken what seemed like everything from me, but my inner determination was not going to let it take my hope. I believe I had to learn life lessons along the way for me to transform into the person I have become today. David taught me to never give up on hope long before I started my self-healing journey.

During the ten months of eagerly anticipating whether we would find David or not, all I had was my hope and faith. I had nothing else, I just had to believe, which I did. The fantastic thing about hope is nobody can take it from you unless you let them. The whole world can be falling apart around you yet, you can still choose to feel hopeful that things can improve. Hope is sincerely yours, and there is something so special about that.

The Turning Point

January 2019 was a significant turning point in my life. Christmas 2018 had left me shattered and my soul longed for something, anything to make this journey easier. Sometimes things must get worse before they get better. There was something immensely influential in the pain I experienced that Christmas. It was like a light switch went off, and something clicked within me. I realised I needed to change. This time I was aware that the change needed to come from me and no one else. It was the first time since losing David I was willing to let go of control and surrender to my grief. I had enough; I did not know how, but I needed David to help me.

On New Year's Day, I visited David's grave. I sat and cried and poured my soul out to him. I let go of the control that had a tight grip on my grief. It felt so heavy, and I had become weary of clinging onto it so tightly. Instead, I begged David to help me. I had done this thousands of times, but something was different. On that day, I truly meant it.

By surrendering my grief that day, I gave David and the angels permission to intervene and help me. I told him I would do whatever I had to do to make this easier. I just needed David's guidance on where to start. Instantly I felt relieved; I got this overwhelming feeling of being supported and a burst of warm energy embraced my heart. For the first time, I think I accepted myself exactly where I was at. I accepted that David was gone and that he was not coming back. The resistance I was holding onto, I let go. I accepted that at that moment, I was lost, alone, scared, broken and fragile. I sat there and cried in total presence of exactly how I felt at that moment.

I felt relieved as I sat in the empty graveyard; I felt an inner strength wash over me. I knew he was pushing me on giving me the courage I needed.

This time change had to start with me, no one else. Before this, I was continually looking for others to help fix me. I would have tried anything bar helping myself, that indeed was just too much effort. I thought the world owed me something. I was waiting for someone to come and put me back together. On that day, it became apparent to me, the only one who could fix my situation, was me. Everything started and ended with me. I was now willing to try to help myself, and that was a significant achievement.

Life was passing me by. I could not handle any more pain. I was still so young; there was no way I was facing another Christmas feeling like that. David certainly would not have wanted me to. I thought about all the labels I had attached to my grief. Up until that day, I had consciously decided my life had ended, that life as I knew it was over and, in one way, that was the truth. The life I was familiar with was over, but life still existed. I still existed.

To the outer world, I may have looked like I was coping. Inside, I was a shell of myself. I had no real taste for life. I just felt like I had to get on with it. I cannot explain, but I could not do it anymore. I needed a bit of joy in my life. I did not know how I was going to do it, but the difference was I was prepared to try, and that was a huge turning point in my life.

It was time to test the labels I had put on my grief. I was ready to live rather than just survive; I needed to. Sometimes, our situation must get worse before it can get better. There was such power in those two weeks over Christmas. I had no distractions; I had no choice but to feel all the emotions in my body. The energy in that pain pushed me on to try and claim my life back.

I was not moving on, rather I was moving forward. The most significant barrier in my grief was the fact I thought doing anything positive meant that I was moving on. Instead of using the term 'moving on', I was going to call it 'moving forward'. 'Moving on' sends shivers down my spine, like I was leaving David behind. He was making one thing noticeably clear he was coming with me wherever I went and that was for sure.

I feel that you do not just move on; you move forward and adapt to the new tides of life. I am no grief guru, but I had begun to learn that resisting the winds of change was a lot harder than going with the flow of change.

Grief does turn your life upside down. It makes you feel like you have little control. At times you can feel very unsafe. It also became apparent to me that even though I felt I had little control; I always had a choice. Something I felt for so long I did not have. Now I had made a choice. I just needed to implement positive changes in my life.

My New Year's Resolution

My first new year's resolution of 2019 was to change my attitude towards my job. I was not giving it a fair chance at all. Before the accident I always loved my jobs. I loved helping people it gave me a purpose and a reason to get up in the morning.

It was time to stop feeling so sorry for myself. I was going to give myself a break and cut myself some slack. I was pushing forward, empowering myself to make changes to make life more tolerable. It's bizarre what a change in perspective can do; within a few weeks, I could notice the positive changes it was having. I started to see work was an incredibly positive outlet for me. It gave me a purpose and a focus again, where for so long I did not have one. The difference was at the time I did not want one. I was still heartbroken, but I was determined and I was really trying. I was aware of how my attitude and my thoughts were going to play a massive part in this 'moving forward'.

I was reaping the rewards of my new attitude and perspective towards life. The grief had by no means gone away, but my mindset was changing. I was starting to treat my mind and body with the respect it deserved. I even started trying to eat healthily and incorporate more exercise into my lifestyle. I could not put my finger on it, but I had a yearning like I was searching for something more in life.

I was still getting notes from Sophie, and through the notes, he kept telling me how proud he was of me. For the first time in a long time, I started to begin to feel proud of myself too

The Teacher Shall Appear When the Student is Ready

Just before Christmas, I had attended a few reiki sessions. I did not know much about it before I tried it, at that time I was willing to try anything. Reiki is an ancient energy healing practice. It involves a hands-on healing technique. After my first session, I felt a deep sense of calm and I felt very relaxed. I was amazed, as before the session, I felt in utter chaos.

I returned for another reiki session in 2019. This session was different from the other sessions I had received. I had been asking David for guidance on the next steps I needed to take. On that day, I was told exactly what I needed to do, whether I liked it or not. I had been asking for the answers now it was time to receive them.

The closest way to describe this lady is she is like a walking angel. I know on that day David sent her to give me the divine guidance I needed. After my reiki session, she sat me down and told me I had two options in life.

I could go down one path, where what happened to David would define my life. I would believe life served me a great injustice. Instead of trying to build myself a life, one which David would have wanted for me, I would let guilt and fear take over. I would hold myself back from positive experiences in life. Instead of living here, I would just survive.

Or I could choose to take the second path. I could start seeing the positives in my life and start creating a future for myself'. I still did not want a life without David; of course, I didn't? If I had a magic wand, I would go straight back to my life in Canada. I was very aware this was not going to happen. I needed to do more here than just survive. My soul was craving something so much more. She then asked me a question that stopped me in my tracks, "What kind of future can you see?" I remember looking at her in dismay. I was listening and taking it all in. I did not have an answer for that question because I had never thought that far ahead.

For a second, a part of me believed it would be easier just to keep feeling sorry for myself. Questions like that were too hard to answer. A future without David was not worth thinking about. I thought about if it was the other way around and I was gone and David was here. It would have pained me to see him suffering like this. I would have done anything for him to bring some joy back into his life. The grief I carried was defining who I was. That one question brought up feelings of enormous anxiety and guilt. I wondered 'what am I doing even entertaining this question? Do I even love David if I am willing to try and make positive changes in my life?' Of course, I loved him. I knew that, and so did he. Your mind though has a funny way of playing tricks on you.

I was advised on my way home to go and buy a journal. I was to write down a vision of what I wanted my future to look like. My future, a future without him here in the physical sense. I had previously closed my mind to this. Now, it was time to try to become more receptive and create a new vision. An exercise like this was a way of using visualisation to send a different message to the brain. One that said 'hello I'm still here'.

I kept thinking of the first option where I would survive the rest of my life. It was probably a little bit dramatic, but I imagined living alone growing old with far too many cats, everyone one else living their life and me just waiting to kick the bucket. Now, that was not one bit dramatic! Honestly, at the time that was precisely how I felt my life could go.

I could imagine David looking down sighing at the life I had just wasted.

I knew David did not want that for me. It was becoming apparent that a part of me did not want that either. I felt like on that day he was intervening and that I had just had a divinely guided intervention. Now it was time for me to do the work. I cried the whole way home in the car, but that was not unusual. The music I was listening to would draw tears from a stone. I had a habit of listening to David's funeral songs on repeat, not the best idea yet a common occurrence. Music had a way of empathising with me; often, I felt like the lyrics spoke to my soul.

Listening to the Divine Guidance

I stopped in the shop and bought a small notepad. I picked a nice pink one and little did I know on that day how special that little notepad would become. I was still living at home with my parents. I remember walking in the front door and going upstairs. I knew I had to do it straight away, or I would reconsider if I thought about it too much. I felt so much shame and fear for what I was about to do. I decided to pick the bathroom of all places, purely because I could lock the door.

The guilt began to overpower me. How could I plan for my future, what would David say? I knew I had to push through and just do it. A force bigger than me was pushing me on and sparking this determination. I sat on the cold bathroom floor for ages as I attempted to put pen to paper. The anxiety would then kick in and I would drop the pen as quick as I picked it up. How was I going to do this? Everything I wanted in my life was with David. We had a plan already. I was so torn, I felt like I was at a crossroads I needed life to get a bit better, but at the same time I was not ready to let any piece of David go. So, what did I know? I knew David was not coming back. I knew I had to try to start to navigate this new life.

Eventually, I got courageous and started to write. 'What did I want from this new life that I was trying to navigate? Who was Ciara without David? Who did she want to be? What did she want to do?'

I always loved the saying 'it was not the life I chose' I certainly did not choose this life, but it was clear that right now I did have a choice. I could either move with change or be resistant and fight against it. Change is scary; even the smallest of changes can spark turmoil or uncertainty within us. Change means movement into the unknown and a loss of control.

In that moment I chose to change and I began to think about my new life. The one thing I always knew was that I wanted children, so I wrote that down. Tears rolled down my face as I wrote on the page. I used to have David plagued talking about our little family and all the kids we were going to have. My mind started to race with lots of irrational thoughts. I thought about how there was nothing stopping me going ahead and trying to start a family on my own. However, this wouldn't be realistic and after all, I still had all this grief to deal with. At that moment, I could not envisage ever meeting anyone else never mind the thought of having children with them. For now, I would write down, 'I would like to have children' and let David plan the rest.

I was making progress. I was thinking; I was visioning a future for myself. I had never let myself do that before, it was so hard, but I was doing it. It was a start, and I had to start somewhere. For now, the immaculate conception sat better with me than the thought of having children with another man. I also decided I would like to move out of my parents' house. I needed to gain some of my independence back. I wrote down on my little pink notepad that Hope and I would move out.

I then got this urge to complete a Reiki course and wrote that down too. Reiki was helping me and I was interested in completing the course. My intuition led me to feel that David was guiding me towards it in recent weeks, as it kept being brought to my attention.

The reiki course seemed the most realistic option. I was going to try and organise that straight away. I was pretty certain if I told anyone I was thinking of having a baby, interventions would have been held quick enough. I felt a release writing all that down. It was like there was a little devil on one shoulder and an angel on the other, with very conflicting viewpoints. Later in my journey, I was made aware that my ego was one of these sides holding me back. My ego was thriving in this identity I had built with my grief. The other side was my spirit which was happy I was following my rightful path. I was listening to my intuition and my inner nudges.

Confirmation from the Angels

I closed the notepad and decided to seek guidance by picking a few angel cards. I always sought great comfort from these and they had become one of my daily rituals. I knew through these David always sent me the messages I needed.

The first card I picked was the children card. I could not believe it and tears rolled down my face. I knew this was confirmation telling me I was going to have children, that I was always destined to be a mother in this lifetime. He knew me better than anyone else; he knew ever since we met, I longed for this. It also made me feel so supported knowing that David was with me and guiding me through this. I may have felt alone, but he was there right beside me.

I felt sad because I had always imagined having my happy family with him still, I continued on and picked another card. The next card I got was the steady progress card. This card read that the angels were acknowledging the work I was putting into myself. This card touched me because I knew more than ever; this was David pushing me on. He knew how hard I was finding this, but he was with me every step of the way.

The next card touched me on a whole other level and sparked a bit of frustration in me. I picked out the wedding card. I knew this was David's way of saying that I was going to meet someone one day and have the family unit I longed for. I remember rolling up into a ball on the floor. I cradled myself like a baby just to give myself some comfort. This was so hard, but at the same time, I felt like he was right there beside me egging me on. I swore up to David. The thought of ever letting anyone into my life like that scared me to the point that I completely dismissed it. For now, in my eyes, that was not an option. I knew none of this was going to be easy.

Finding out who Ciara was and Finding Reiki

I felt like we had just started operation two, the journey to find who Ciara is without David. Operation one was to find David; he showed us many times how he was leading that journey. Operation one was completed with flying colours. In completing operation one, David equipped me with the skills I needed for operation two. David showed me the inner strength, determination and resilience I had buried within me to overcome any obstacle thrown at me. With everything I had been through, surely finding Ciara could not be that hard.

I rang 'Sophie' and told her straight away what had just happened. After all my crying, I felt focused. Sophie said to me that David was pushing me on. She told me 'I was ready.' That day was a huge turning point for me. It was the first time I let myself envisage a future without David.

I had booked to do a Reiki course at the end of 2018 and I ended up cancelling it. Reflecting, I was not ready for it; I think divine timing kicked in. The second time around, I was ready and I felt I was being guided to exactly where I needed to be.

The weekend I spent completing my Reiki Level One; I laughed, I cried and shared intimate moments with people I had never met before. It did not feel one bit strange; it felt perfect. For someone who had been crippled with anxiety, especially when it came to anything new, this surprised me. I felt so comfortable. More importantly, I felt something alter within my soul, a passion within me wanting to come out.

The days involved a lot of meditation, something that was very new to me. I was surprised at how much I enjoyed it. I always thought my mind would be far too busy to meditate. I had this misconception that it was only for hippie people, people who did not have a care in the world. How wrong I was, as after I experienced it, I felt silly for the judgement I had placed on it.

Meditation was magnificent, opening my eyes to a whole new world. A world that is enchanting and magical. I realised I could connect with David on an even deeper level through meditation. I knew so little about reiki before this yet something about it sent a passion into my soul. For so long, I felt like the fire within me was extinguished, but it was starting to flicker again. Throughout the weekend, I felt like I was remembering, rather than learning something new. I was starting to delve into spirituality; I needed to find a deeper meaning to life. I was so open to everything. I needed to know more. I was willing and wanted to learn more about spirituality and how it could help me process what had happened in my life.

After the first day, I was so happy; I had not felt like that in such a long time. I rang my friend and told her I had the most fantastic time. She could hear it in my voice. I could not wait to return. I was only doing the course for my self-development, but something told me David had other plans for me. I also rang Sophie. I was ecstatic on the phone she could feel my energy. She told me David was excited too and had plans for me, but I didn't need her confirmation to tell me this because I already knew.

Meditating my Mind & Connecting to my Spirit Guides

The second day I eagerly returned. I was delighted to hear we would be doing more meditation. As I felt my eyes close, I felt so supported, connected and loved. I felt that I was part of something so much bigger than myself. Something told my soul that this was precisely what it needed. My head, however, kept trying to figure out what was going on.

I felt like I did so much healing, gaining this new awareness. I was made aware that we all have spirit guides who watch over and protect us. If someone told me three years ago, I would be communicating with my spirit guides or even believed in such a thing it would have brought me great entertainment. I would have thought they were delusional and disregarded it.

Our spirit guides are always there to help us. We can call on them in any situation. The only thing is they cannot help us if we do not ask them. They would jump at the chance to help us but because we have free will, we must ask for their support. There was no logic to any of this; again, I had to trust my heart and intuition. I left that weekend thinking everyone needs to do Reiki Level One. That weekend intrigued me to look even deeper into the angelic world, into meditation, spirituality - anything that might give a deeper meaning to my life.

Finding Positive Affirmations and Gratitude

I started to see how I was growing and transforming as a person. I felt like a little seed that was starting to water itself. I became determined to keep learning and growing. The more enthusiastic I became, the more I started looking into new tools to help me advance. I noticed quickly that whenever I needed to learn something, I would be redirected to a video or a book that answered my query or equipped me with the knowledge I needed.

The next tool that was sent to me were positive affirmations. I had heard of them previously. I discovered later in my journey how significant and influential they could be. Positive affirmations are positive statements that can help you overcome challenging thoughts and beliefs you may have. You repeat them often to get the desired results. I became fascinated with how the mind works. Every time we say something, we are affirming that to be true. At first, I thought, 'wow, I have a lot of reprogramming to do with all the negative thoughts I had been affirming'.

Up to this point, I was continually affirming to myself 'I can't do this. I am grief, and this is not getting any easier'. One video I watched compared our mind to a typewriter. Our thoughts are the words we send to the typewriter. The only answer the typewriter ever gives is 'ok'. Now that is glorious if you are affirming positive thoughts. I think it is safe to say we are often our own worst critic. The stuff we tell ourselves we wouldn't dream of saying to another human being; I would not have back then anyway.

For so long, I had been affirming that 'this is not getting any easier'. The universe was then, in turn, sending me more challenges to make everything more complicated. When I got an understanding of positive affirmations, I became very mindful of the way I spoke to myself. I was excited to use this tool to try and rewire some of the beliefs I had been programming my mind with.

I was aware that it was not going to happen overnight. Here is where determined Ciara came in, David had taught me so well. I had experienced a glimmer of joy from what the reiki course had given me. More than anything, I wanted to feel more of it. I needed it in my life; my soul craved it.

I decided my first positive affirmation would be 'I am joyful'. Starting, I remember feeling a bit silly stating 'I am joyful'. One morning, I found it incredibly difficult. I woke up feeling angry with the world; joy was not exactly on my priority list. The determination in me proceeded to say the three words. I knew I was a work in progress, I had to keep going even if, on that day, I did not want too. Another day I decided to put a bit of feeling into it. I had read somewhere; this makes the affirmations even more powerful. My new motto was 'let's fake it until you make it'.

I still felt guilty and often wondered what David would think. Deep in my heart, I knew that he was the one who was sending me these new tools, he wanted me to live again. At times, I was still so hard on myself. I would feel so bad for wanting to feel better. I needed to give myself a break, and with that my second affirmation came to be 'I am strong, I can do this'. Of course, I was strong. Look at all I had been through;

everyone else could see this except me. It was time to change that.

The next thing I incorporated into my daily lifestyle was gratitude. In the beginning, I found this quite tricky. I knew I was grateful for my family and friends, but the smaller things in life seemed to pass me by entirely. After practicing gratitude for a short period, I could see the magical effects it could have. It made me become present and aware of all the beauty that surrounds us.

One day, I remember waking up feeling grateful for being alive and breathing. I remember meaning it and getting a warm fuzzy feeling in my heart. It gave me a reason to pause for a second. I was able to see how far I had come in the last few months. It made me feel so excited and determined; I could see the changes in myself and I wanted to keep flourishing. I could finally see how lucky I really was. I wanted to be here. I wanted to be here alive and breathing. I was finally starting to live my life again.

Making Healthy Routines

I had now been off antidepressants for a few months, and my mind was feeling clearer. I was aware my body needed as much attention as my mind. I knew I had put weight on and for a long time I was in denial of just how much weight. To my shock, I had put on four and a half stone. The reality of this was enough to give me the kick in the right direction that I needed. It was time to curb what I was eating and try and incorporate more exercise into my day. I was starting to see the link between the mind, body, and soul and I needed to work on all three actively. Every morning I would do some meditation, practice gratitude and do some of my positive affirmations. I also tried to commit to getting some form of physical activity throughout the day.

One morning, I nearly danced into the office. I was bursting with joy after my morning routine and it was not even 10am. I had gone for a run, done some meditation, practiced gratitude and done my positive affirmations. I was relishing in my newfound routine; my body and soul were singing. For the first time in a long time, I was looking after myself. Who was this woman because I sure didn't know her? It felt so good to start caring about myself. The little things I had been doing were having a massive impact on my life.

As I sat at my desk that morning, I thought about the nicest vision I had while meditating. It was of me kicking a football to David. I sat there and thought about how real it felt; it made my heart feel so warm and full. I wanted to tell someone about my experience. Our love was still there. I remained quiet; instead, I just relished my newfound connection with David in spirit. Meditation started opening doors for me that I thought were locked. I felt so connected with David and my angels. They kept telling me I was on the right path. I saw a whole new world and I wanted to shout it from the rooftops. Of everything that I was incorporating into my life, I felt meditation was having a profound effect on me. Every time I meditated, I felt like my soul was saying 'thank you' it felt soothing like I was at home.

In those few months, my life was changing all around me. I was doing things I never thought possible. I had completed a Reiki Level One course; I was building myself up with positive affirmations and I was meditating. I had also started to lose some weight. I felt like I was beginning to flourish. Self-love was next on my list, this being the idea that we should love and care for ourselves unconditionally. I knew one thing, for the first time in my whole life, I was starting to have a better relationship with myself.

I was navigating my self-healing journey, and it felt so empowering, except I didn't feel alone because not only did I have David guiding me now, I also had my spirit guides. I became aware that I was going through a spiritual awakening. The more I investigated it; I discovered that it is more common for people who have been through trauma in their life to experience this. The trauma pushes you to the darkest place in your life. To find a way out, you need to find meaning to your life, your purpose and the reason why you were sent here. It is often referred to 'as waking up'. This summed up how

I felt, and I was starting to understand what was going on for me.

Acknowledging the Grief

I was fully aware that the grief was never going to go away; I didn't want it to either. The grief was the love I had and continued to have for David. This time, I had all the tools in my toolbox and I was prepared. Some days all the meditation in the world or positive affirmations did not kick that feeling I got from grief. At first, this frustrated me; I would be so judgmental asking 'why is the meditation not working?' I then realised I just needed to sit with my pain, with no judgements and feel it and let it be.

I started to realise that the grief was not the giant evil monster I was viewing it as. I began to notice a pattern that if I did not acknowledge the suffering, it would come back fighting twice as hard. I had to acknowledge it. I had to give it space, to sit with it and let it be for it too served a purpose.

At times, I was afraid the grief would come back and consume me like it had before; this caused me a lot of anxiety. It was like there was a constant battle between me and the grief. I might let the grief win for a weekend, a day, an hour, but I would always brush myself off and put my armour back on again for battle. I was in it for the long haul. I was going to fight this grief. I was not willing to go back to the place I was before. I was moving forward with David in my heart.

For the first time since losing David, I wanted to find who Ciara was without David. A part of me sometimes wondered did I even know who Ciara was when he was here. I was starting to accept myself, even the grief. For a long time, I had so little respect for my body, but now I was starting to listen to it and give it what it needed. Through studying reiki, I became aware of how smart our bodies are. Our bodies will tell us exactly what they need. But, more often than not, we do not listen.

I was making significant progress; I could visibly see and feel the changes within myself. I was a work in progress, just as the saying goes 'Rome wasn't built in a day'.

I was becoming more self-aware, which was helping me make massive leaps in the right direction.

If I felt sad, I let myself feel sad. If I felt angry, I let myself feel angry. I always tried to put a spin on it that tomorrow would be a better day. Sometimes I would have to write the whole weekend off and curl into a ball and just rest. As I said before, our bodies know what they need, it is our job to listen. On my bad days, I sat through the pain. I journaled and wrote down my feelings. Sometimes I was too annoyed to journal, so I just watched videos of David on repeat. I would cry until I had no tears left to cry. In those moments, life was overwhelming, raw and very painful and I was very engrossed in my grief. Afterwards, I started to notice that when I gave the pain the time it needed, I felt better for it. I felt like I did some healing and let out some repressed emotions.

Finding Me

By May 2019, I had gone five months into my self-healing journey and I was reaping the rewards of my daily routine. I was starting to figure out who Ciara was without David. I had just completed my Reiki Level Two course. This meant I could practice as a Reiki Practitioner. I was passionate about reiki because it involved helping others open up to their self-healing abilities. I had seen the positive impact it had on me and I wanted to be able to offer this healing to others.

I felt like I finally had a purpose and I was trying to express myself in any way possible. I had even started writing poetry something which took me by surprise. With each poem I wrote, I felt like it came straight from my soul. The inspiration would hit me randomly just to write; afterwards, it felt like I had given my soul permission to create and just be. I liked who this Ciara was becoming.

Through Sophie, David told me he wanted me to write a book. This message sparked confusion within me. 'How would I be able to write a book?' I was still figuring things out for myself. It sparked something within my intuition that led me to believe that down the line; this could be a possibility.

Alighting a Passion Within Me

Over the years, David would have always tried to encourage me and help me find something I was passionate about. This often would have been met with frustration from me. David knew how important it was to be passionate about something. His passion for football ran through his veins. It was beautiful to witness. David could see me pick up hobbies and then forget about them after a while. He wanted me to be as passionate about something in this lifetime as he was about football.

For what felt like the first time in my life, I was feeling passionate too. I felt passionate about using everything I had learnt to become the best version of myself. I felt passionate about one day sharing this wisdom to help others. I felt passionate about healing, growing and evolving.

I had been stripped of my identity; I had been given a clean slate -something I viewed for so long as a negative I was starting to view as a positive. I could now choose who I wanted to be and what I wanted to do.

Life is too short to care what other people think, and it is precious, something I knew only too well. I was learning I needed to be my authentic self and continue what I was doing.

Embracing the Changes and Creating a New Story

I started to view people and the world differently. In the world we live in we can often be quick to judge others. Through my journey, I was starting to realise that we are all the same; we are all one. We all came here for one reason, one purpose, to spread love. I put all my effort into changing and growing. Through meditation, journaling and spending lots of time out in nature, I was gaining my identity again and this time it felt like me. Whilst reflecting on this, I thought not only would David have preferred this Ciara I was starting to prefer her too.

I started seeing the magic and enchantment of being able to create a new script for my life. I began to amplify my positive affirmations. I had been doing them daily anyway, but this time I was putting more feeling into them. I will never forget one specific day whilst I was out driving in my car, an overpowering feeling came over me. I knew it was joy. I started to cry, but they were not tears of sadness, they were tears of joy.

In that moment nothing in my life had changed, nothing. I didn't win the lottery or get fantastic news. What had changed was the fact I had chosen me. I had decided to live again and create a life that was worth living. In that moment life could not have been any better.

It made me think about the society we live in; we are nearly programmed that things will only improve when we receive external validation, for example, when you get that job or meet that new partner etc.
I saw and felt first-hand this was not the case. Ok, of course, these things all help but the real changes and

magic must come from within. It is the best feeling in the world. That day, I sat in that bliss of joy, knowing the only reason I was there was because of all the growth and inner work I was doing.

If you are always looking for outside validation to fulfil you, you may end up going around in circles figuratively speaking, continually looking for something when all your answers lay within.

Channeling my Inner Being

I was still getting uplifting messages from David nearly every day channeled through Sophie. It was evident that she was stepping back, she kept telling me 'you've got this'.

One day, I decided to channel my own message from David. I closed my eyes for a few minutes and asked him to give me a message. I opened my eyes, put the pen to paper and just wrote. I felt the pen move faster, as I wrote on the page. This process is called automatic writing. Again, I had no logic for this, but I had a heart full of faith and trust. My intuition led me to believe it was exactly what I needed to do.

That note was the start of many; anytime I needed guidance, I would use automatic writing and get advice from David. We can all do this; you just must have faith and believe—our loved ones in spirit love when we try and reach out and connect with them.

Shedding with the Seasons

By summertime, I felt like I had shed a few layers of grief and that I was emerging into an improved version of myself. Next on my list was to go travelling solo. I had booked to go to Melbourne to visit my friend and then onto Vietnam to see my sister.

I was looking forward to seeing them, but I was also terrified. I had never really travelled by myself, especially a journey that long. David and I loved travelling, so this was a big deal for me. I was independently embracing life and going back to doing something I loved to do. In the early days, I often wondered, would my love for travel ever come back.

The week before I was due to go, I could see the progress I had made. I was excited to embark on an adventure. This time there was no shame or guilt; I deserved and needed a break away. Visually, I was going alone, but I knew this was far from the truth. David and I had discussed that at some stage in our lifetime, we would travel to Australia. It was on our bucket list; little did we know then we would be travelling there together as close as ever but also worlds apart.

The day before I was due to set off travelling, I went back to my Reiki Practitioner for a reiki session. She told me she could see a difference in my energy; this made my eyes light up. I felt so much lighter I knew I had changed. Instead of feeling shame or guilt at hearing this, I felt alive and excited. All my hard work was paying off.

I was reaping the rewards. Instead of the grief weighing me down, it was coming along with me on this new journey. Before I left, she told me to make sure to bring a journal with me on my travels and I knew that was another confirmation from David that I was going to write this book.

I thought back to one of the days after David's memorial mass. I remembered being at home with my family. The Mayo match was playing on the television, blaring as loud as anything. I could not stand to watch or listen to it as the pain was too intense. All it did was emphasise the fact that David was no longer here. I felt robbed as he should have been there watching it with us.

Eventually, I had to leave the kitchen; all I wanted to do was scream. I went up to my bedroom and cried. I got an urge to write, so that is precisely what I did. I took myself back to the moment I heard about David's accident and put all my feelings and thoughts down on paper.

I did not know why I started to write, but I did. For a moment, it offered me a little bit of relief. As I wrote, it felt like my mind was trying to figure out how I got into this mess and somehow try to get a handle on it. It felt like instead of keeping all my thoughts stuck inside of me, I let a few out. As I wrote I cried, I did not sugarcoat how I was feeling I just jotted it down word for word. One day David's Dad accidentally read it. I remember him telling me I had a way with words. At the time, it provided me with a bit of humour. I also felt a little bit mortified that he had found it. It was never my intention for anyone to read that, but me.

To me, it was a way of letting my emotions out. A part of me lavished in the compliment of my writing. I scraped through English in school. I was not the academic type, this was different, I was not using my imagination; I was writing about my most profound purest emotion, my life. I was writing from my soul, it was pure, and it was honest.

For a moment, I wondered, what was the reason I was dealt these cards, was it to help others? If David wanted me to write a book, he was going to have to lead the way.

I wanted to give myself a hug. I thought back to that fragile girl that was me. So lost and afraid, entirely out of her depth. I wished I could have told her everything was going to be ok. She had so many people around her trying to support her, yet, she felt so alone. I longed to go back and tell her she was so brave and strong. She was a warrior; everyone could see this except her. I shed a tear for her but then awoke to the fact that I needed to be there in that dark place to get to where I was today. My life had gone full circle, something which seemed so unimaginable for so long. Here I was questioning even writing a book to help others.

I felt gratitude for that dark place because without being there, I would never have got to where I am today. Everything serves a purpose in our lives.

This new Ciara showed herself love, she creatively expressed herself, this new Ciara was more at home than she had ever felt in her whole life. I was getting a unique taste for life and the magic that surrounds all of us.

I thought back to before David's accident, I thought of how anxious or how annoyed I got at trivial things that in the scheme of life have no importance whatsoever. The one thing I had learnt was that every day was a blessing.

My Divinely Guided Journey

I was calm and collected as I headed off on my new adventure. That was until the bus got delayed on the way to the airport. I started to work up a sweat; negative thoughts began to loom in my head. I told myself 'I can't even make it to the airport.' I thought back to when David and I would have previously gone on holidays. He would've always been the organised one. I had it easy; all I had to do was turn up.

It was time to reframe my negative thoughts, 'look at how far I had come! Of course, I was able for this! Sure, I was not alone; I had David'. I sucked it up and just prayed to him to help settle my mind and to help me sort things out. When I thought about the worst thing that could happen, which was that I would miss my flight, I started to feel a little silly in the scheme of things; it wasn't a big deal. In that moment, I wanted everything to run smoothly.

You can imagine my delight getting through the other side, waiting to board. I felt like a queen and was so proud of myself, 'task one complete, David we have got this'. I had my fresh new journal with me. I was ready to take on whatever David was willing to throw at me. I remember, at this stage, nothing at all surprised me. My first stop was Melbourne in Australia. I was so excited to see my friend who had moved over there a few years ago. I got through the first flight to Dubai, no hassle. In Dubai Airport I got this pang of fear and anxiety, 'what was I doing?' It was so hot in the airport; it was overbearing. I felt completely out of my depth. As

I walked around in the blazing heat, I started to feel so lonely.

I watched on as a couple affectionately embraced each other. I wondered what I was doing heading on an adventure by myself. I was not ready for this. Again, my most prominent critic was coming out, which was me. I had a little cry in the bathroom and brushed myself off. I sat in the terminal and wrote in my journal and prayed to the angels.

As I waited to board the plane, I put my earphones in and listened to a guided meditation, that seemed to ease my anxiety for a little bit.

I was going to squeeze my friend when I saw her. I felt uplifted as I knew I was on the second leg of the journey. As I got onto the plane, I made my way down to my seat. I was sitting in the back row with only two seats and extra legroom. Looking down, I mumbled 'thank you, David'.

When I sat down, an older man sat beside me. He informed me that he was due to sit somewhere else and was going to see would someone swap seats with him. Luckily enough for him, the person agreed. I thought it was strange how he randomly ended up switching seats. My conclusion was David had sensed I was lonely and sent this man in to talk to me.

I had not spoken to anyone for a few hours except to say hello to the flight attendants on the plane. It was so lovely. I think he needed to talk to someone just as much as I did. At one stage, I had fallen asleep; when I awoke, he had kept the food for me that they had handed out. It was like David had sent him to mind me. We spoke for most of the journey, which made the flight fly by. He was an exceedingly kind person and you could tell he had a kind heart.

When we landed in Melbourne, we walked from the plane to immigration together. When we got to the self-service immigration booth, my passport would not work, so I had to go to the desk. When I spoke to the police officer, he asked me was I travelling alone, and I replied 'yes'.

My friend from the flight came up beside me and asked me was everything ok, and I replied 'yes'. They then asked him did we know each other, and he replied 'yes'. So, for a second, it looked like I was lying. I explained we met on the plane. As I was travelling alone and only in Melbourne for a few days, the police officer informed me that he had some questions he would like to ask. I felt like I was on the border control programme from television. I was under interrogation. The police officer had to speak on the phone to my friend I was visiting before they agreed to let me through immigration. It was extremely stressful, and I remember in my head asking David, 'really?'

It tested my inner strength and resilience, and like everything else I got through it. Walking out of the interrogation room, I wondered had David sent me that challenge to show me how far I had come. I let out a sigh of relief as I noted that my suitcase was the only one left going around on the cart. When I met my friend, we had a great laugh about the situation. I joked that the kind older man probably thought I was a drug lord and I had got caught.

It was clear he was protecting me, but he was also giving me challenges to see how I coped. This story provided great entertainment afterwards and lots of laughs. David continued to show me the inner strength and resilience I had built up.

I Was Exactly Where I Needed to Be

Do you ever just get this feeling that you are exactly where you need to be? I could not put my finger on it, but I was destined to be in Melbourne. All the distractions from home were a million miles away; I could just be me.

I didn't feel lonely; I felt more alive than ever. I made the most of my time here. Every morning I got up and I made sure I meditated. My friend lived in a lovely apartment, which had a balcony. I would sit out and meditate in the brisk cold air. Then I would journal and connect with my angels and David. I was connecting with David and the angels on a much deeper level and it indeed was blissful. I found it easier to connect with them like I had left some of the background noise in Ireland.

The information I was getting was so exciting, and what made things even easier was I could tell my friend all about it. David had planned this journey right down to a tee. He had sent me to someone who understood or who at least was very curious. During my stay, we named ourselves 'the soul sisters' and had many spirituals chats. It was like David had planted me there to gain this knowledge and in doing this, I was also inspiring her. We spoke about how amazing the world is when you figure out that you are never truly alone.

My head was the clearest it had ever felt; I had no distractions; the angels could connect with me easier because I was not continuously distracting myself. I was now accepting what happened on a deeper level. I had made peace that David was gone and never coming back.

It was like the time away allowed me to go to 'soul school', the angels taught me not only did I need to accept what happened I needed to understand why.

I remember one morning channeling a message from David; it said 'Ciara, this was always part of the plan, we chose this to happen'. I remember being told or hearing this before and it sparked a rage in me. 'I chose the love of my life to die because it's the best life journey I have ever been on' (hope you can hear the sarcasm). This time, I felt it deep within and I knew I chose this to happen. What do I mean when I say I chose this? I will try to explain. Before we are born, we all choose a timeline. Nothing happens by chance; there are no coincidences. We have already chosen when we will depart this lifetime before we are born. We also choose the people with whom we are going to connect with in this lifetime. I chose to be with David right up until he died. I chose this so my soul could evolve and grow. I chose this so I could go through all that pain to find a deeper meaning to life. In doing this, I could help others through using my self-healing journey. I was not sad to get this information, I felt relieved, my soul had been given the information, it needed to make peace with all of this. I understood and knew it to be true.

Being with and Accepting 'Me'

One day as I strolled peacefully around Melbourne, I noted that I didn't have as many thoughts as I usually would. In fact, I didn't have many at all. I was in a state of being; I was present. I was not focused on what had happened in my life or where I was going. I was not stuck in the past on what had happened or projecting into the future; I was present relishing in the moment that stood before me.

I had read about it in books, but now I was doing it. I was in a state of appreciation for and of, the present moment. I wanted to scream and shout and tell someone, clearly my ego kicking in! In that moment I had it all, I did not need anything else. I thought back to Ciara before all this happened, being with myself for a few hours would have been a struggle, you could even say a nightmare. The main reason because I didn't love or value myself enough. I thought I needed to be surrounded by people to find happiness. I used to believe if I went shopping and bought 'that' particular item of clothing it would make me happy. If I went on 'that' holiday it would make me happy. I am very aware such things do bring contentment and joy but they only do so for a short period. As I sat at the beach, I analysed my life and realised that I had to have everything taken away from me to learn that everything I needed is within me.

I had found my inner joy and bliss from going deep within, an inner joy and delight that a top or holiday will never fulfil. A feeling that even in chaos we each have a place we can go that is peaceful. To me, it is like going home. I felt freer than I ever felt before. I wished I knew all this before David's death, then I thought even if I did, I probably wouldn't have acted on it. I continued to walk around Melbourne with not a care in the world.

Nothing in my outer life had changed. I was still living at home with my parents, in the same job, no knight in shining armor had tried to rescue me. On the inside everything had changed, I now spoke to myself with love and compassion. I now valued myself and believed I was worthy of all the joy life had to offer. It felt so empowering and I was so proud of myself.

That evening, I met my friend after she finished work. I was eager to tell her about my day. She could see the excitement on my face. I felt so alive and uplifted because I had just let myself 'be'.

'Vibing' High

Since arriving in Melbourne, I felt so energised, inspired and full of joy. I had recently learnt that our energy gives off a natural vibration, our natural state of being is to be in a place of joy or love. I knew I was vibrating high and it felt amazing. When we are in a joyful state of being, the angels and spirits find it easier to connect with us. It was evident, since being in Melbourne, my meditations were a lot more vivid and I felt I was able to connect to the angels on a much deeper level.

One day, while meditating, I got an extraordinary message from Archangel Michael. I had received messages from him before, but this was different, it was powerful. His presence was strong; I could feel his blue light surrounding me. It was so intense; tears streamed down my face. They were not sad tears; they were happy tears. In that moment I felt supported and guided. Archangel Michael told me I was put on this journey to help inspire others and give them hope; he told me it would be through authentically using words to express myself.

I took it as a sign that I had just been given the clarity on what I needed to do. To trust the divine plan that was my life. I believed there was already a plan for me; my next steps were already aligned in the stars. I just had to keep being authentic and being me. I just had to keep learning and loving myself.

Just like that, I embraced my new purpose with open arms. I started to write and the words just flowed. There is something so magical about putting a pen to paper, I was doing it old school. I cannot describe it, but it felt so powerful, I was physically doing the writing, but the inspiration felt so angelic.

With every word that hit the paper, I knew it was divinely guided. David and the angels were writing this book through me. They were using me as a channel.

By now, I was connecting with David regularly through meditation and automatic writing. A part of me longed to see him like Sophie did. I felt like over the last few months I had attended spiritual school and I was embracing it all, I felt like I deserved to see him in the physical sense. I felt so open to it and I would have done anything to make it happen.

Time to Leave Melbourne

It was time to leave Melbourne. I had only been there a few days, but it felt like I had been there a lifetime. My soul felt rested and recharged leaving. I was excited and I was ready to take the next positive step forward.

I knew I had done more healing, I felt it in my soul and that was precisely why David had sent me there. I gained the clarity I needed, I learnt to be present and enjoy life again. Most importantly, I enjoyed positive experiences with my friend. This involved lots of laughter, medicine for the soul.

I seem to keep going back to that quote 'everything happens for a reason'. Initially, my friend was due to travel with me to Vietnam. As I headed off, we laughed knowing David wanted me to embark on this journey by myself.

Next Stop Vietnam

I could not wait to see my sister, to give her a big hug and for her to meet 'new Ciara' and see the progress I had made. She knew me better than anyone; she had seen me at my lowest point. Even when I think back to these times, I wondered how I had got to this new place of appreciation in my life. This is what excited and inspired me more because if I could do it, so could anyone else.

My sister is the most empathetic person I know. After David's accident, she rarely left my side. She was so calm, loving and extremely patient. At the time, the complete opposite of the emotions I was displaying. She put her whole life on pause for me and, often, she was the only person I wanted, which I can imagine put a lot of pressure on her. I needed her and she somehow helped hold whatever pieces of me were left together. She never once judged me; she just remained present. I was too reliant on her.

I thought back to when she told me she was moving to Vietnam, I honestly thought I was not going to cope without her. It suddenly hit me, my sister left at the right time for me and her. Again, David was up there, helping navigate my life. It made me reflect to the exact timing of all the series of events in my life. Everything happened at exactly the right time. I thought back to not being able to find David for ten months. Of course, this was his plan. Everything that happened in my life did so at precisely the right time because he planned it. I had inner dialogue with David after my 'aha moment', I laughed and said "David, you know what? I'm ready, send me whatever you think I need".

Looking Good from the Outside In

It was so lovely to see my sister and I cherished the time we spent together. She too, could see the changes, but more importantly, she could see how inspired I was. I kept telling her 'everything we need is within us to heal and grow' and I told her my plan for writing a book.

In the mornings, I continued to meditate and write. I felt creative and inspired in doing so. Every time I closed my eyes to meditate, I felt more at home than I did anywhere else. I remember one day sitting on the balcony and I asked David for a sign. I wondered if I was really going to write a book. If so, how do I enlighten and share the wisdom I have learnt with others.

As I sat on the balcony basking in the sun, out of nowhere a feather came and hit me straight in the face. My heart instantly felt vibrant and full. In that moment I felt so supported, loved and guided. I felt as if a hundred angels were surrounding me, giving me the clarity and answers I needed.

I ran to tell my sister about the feather. She could see the joy in my eyes. I was vividly jumping around, holding the feather in my hand. Feeling so empowered I knew this was the confirmation and clarity I needed, I was going to write my book. I continued to write, as I felt more inspired than I ever possibly had. Every time I wrote, a passion alit within me that made me feel alive. I knew this was how David felt about football. I knew he had guided me to find my passion and would continue to do so. I was ready and I was going to do this.

Finding my Purpose

I missed David so much while I was travelling, at the same time, I felt closer to him than ever. Everything just felt right. I knew I had come so far but heading back to Ireland; I knew I had delved even deeper into my spiritual journey. I could see blessings all around me and I had a new found gratitude for the world we live in. I saw the true beauty in life. I made a promise to myself I was going to go back to Ireland and do whatever I had to do to write the book, which happens to be the one you're reading.

Being back in Ireland it hit me I had found my purpose. I was to use my journey to help inspire others to embark on their own healing journey. A healing journey that didn't just involve assisting people in navigating grief but anyone who was dealt with any kind of challenge in their life.

A few days back in Ireland, I remember asking David for another sign. A lorry drove past me and on the number plate were the words GAV. That was David's nickname; most people referred to him as Gav. I was overjoyed and inspired, I felt so connected and I could feel magic all around me. 'Right GAV. Let's do this'.

My Reflections

Grief

Grief is and will always be individual to us; we will all navigate our own journey with it. Grief is not just relevant to our loved ones departing this world. We can grieve a relationship, a job, even entering a new decade of our life, any kind of change or transition can bring up grief. I think this is especially important to signify. For so long, my closest family and friends did not want to tell me their challenges in life as they felt their pain was not justified compared to what I was going through. This is not the case at all and their grief was as important as mine and deserved to be acknowledged and given the time and space.

Grief to me is like an estuary, the water being the emotions of grief. The estuary must let the water/emotions out. Certain events or situations like birthdays or anniversaries can increase the water level (we will compare these to a storm). Over time, the estuary can appear calmer, and the flow is longer, thus the episodes of grief become a lot easier to manage. The grief has not magically disappeared, but you have learnt to incorporate it into your life. You have coping mechanisms. You start to acknowledge your suffering as it is, all the love you have for your deceased loved one. A love that deserves to be recognised, for it will forever hold a place in your heart.

It made me also question how we look at death. Death is the only thing we know to be inevitable. It is the only thing in this life we can be sure of. There are no 'ifs' and 'buts' about it. Yet, it is often treated as somewhat of a taboo. We treat death like it is never going to happen. When it lands on our doorstep, the unimaginable has happened. I wonder if we were educated about death, would it make the pain a little bit easier? Maybe if we had more information or were better prepared for it, the grief process might be a little easier. Perhaps, if as a child or in school, we had conversations about death, it might normalise it. I think it is especially important that we acknowledge death and grief. We educate children in school on everything else, for instance, religion, nutrition, wellbeing, sexual health, yet death is left out.

Making a Connection to our Loved Ones in Spirit

Our loved ones will do anything they can to reach out to us and show us they are still present. If they could reach out and talk to us, they would do so. Do not doubt for a second they are no longer with us. They are.

It is much easier for our loved ones in spirit to connect with us when we are open and willing. You do not have to be skipping around the place, but you must be alert enough or willing to notice the signs if they are put in front of you. They send us any signs they can, numbers, songs, animals etc. In the early days, I might have seen something and thought it was a sign and then dismissed it. The fact you even think that it may be a sign is confirmation that it is. This is where our intuition kicks in. Our intuition is a feeling, a knowing we get, trust this. It is also where faith and trust come in.

In a world where we strive for evidence or logic, where everything we say must be backed up by data or a theory, it is magical to believe in something you simply cannot explain. It brings you back to your childlike essence and the world appears more enchanting. You are surrendering to something out of your control, you are putting your faith in something that you cannot explain.

I know a lot of people struggle with this. I did too for such a long time. It is called letting go of resistance. When we do this, we are giving up our need for needing proof; we are putting our trust into a higher power. There have been many occasions early on where I questioned this. Now I know we are surrounded by our loved ones and angels all the time. In our loneliest hour we are surrounded by more angels than we can even imagine.

I remember one day being in the car and hearing a song saying 'Ciara, Ciara, Ciara', I got so emotional; tears were streaming down my face. I had no proof, but I knew it was David. Music is so powerful and has a powerful means to connect with you. Be alert and listen to the music surrounding you. Listen to the lyrics as they often have hidden messages in them just for you. Your signs will be individual to you and there is no right or wrong way. Trust your heart and intuition.

Graciously Granted a Miracle

If you take nothing from this book other than gaining a sense of awe that miracles do happen, that will be enough for me. I keep thinking back to the second time we left the lake after being told we had to cease the search for David.

In that moment I could have given up, but I believed that we would find David and bring him home. I had no evidence to believe this would be a possibility, if anything, all the evidence was showing us otherwise, but I refused to give up. I knew it would be a miracle if we found him. But I believed and that was the difference. I believed when others told me to be rational; I did not care if they all thought I was naïve. I wonder did my soul and my intuition know all along because I was adamant, we were going to find him.

I had no evidence, just a feeling in my heart and my gut. I listened to it, and I was not afraid to tell anyone who tried to dampen my spirits; they were wrong. The one thing I could not afford to lose was hope. If I lost hope, I lost everything. So, I held onto that hope with everything and we did it, we found him with faith and love and a lot of tears. It was a miracle and it took me a long time to see it but every second of the day miracles are happening all around us. We just need to be willing to open our eyes and see them.

'I Chose Me'

Through my self-development and self-reflection, I think the reason I got to where I am today is because I made a choice. I chose me. If I could put another stage in the typical grief stages, we read in psychology books, I would put, 'choice' in. I know acceptance is one and it is essential, but it is the next step of choosing to adapt to this new life that's when the changes I felt became more evident. Acceptance means you have made peace with what has happened. I think for a long time, I became stuck in acceptance. I had accepted what had happened, but I did not know how to move forward with this new found acceptance. I think this is symbolic of any challenge in life and not just grief.

I am not going to lie and say it was easy because it was so, so hard. But never underestimate how strong you are, no matter what challenges life throws at you. To 'choose' does not mean to simply move on or forget about your loved one, it means you choose to navigate this new life. That is all our loved ones in spirit want for us. To try and adapt to this new life, in which they will be with us every step of the way. Choose you because you deserve it, choose you because you are beautiful, choose you because you are loved and protected.

I had to go inwards to find all the clarity and answers I needed. It took time and perseverance and I nearly lost my way on more than a few occasions. Going inwards changes your perspective on everything. You realise that love is all we are. You understand that the only person you can control in this life is you. Put all your effort into yourself, in doing so your whole world around you changes for the better. Life slows down, and instead of living in the future or the past, we begin to live as much as we can in the present moment.

Incorporating a daily self-care routine and changing my mindset were fundamental in getting me to where I am today. I mentioned previously I became fascinated by the active role our minds play in helping us heal and grow. We feed our minds every second of the day. Every day we are manifesting thoughts into our outer reality. The beautiful thing is we can decide at any moment to take control of our minds and when we do, I promise you it is the most magical feeling you will ever get. It can be as simple as just being a little more aware of your daily thinking patterns.

There is also a great link between our mind and our physical body. To give you an example, compare your mind and physical body to a car with a dodgy engine. Your physical body is 'the car' and the dodgy engine is your mind. You can continue to fix the vehicle and all the other aspects in it. However, unless you get to the root of the dodgy engine, more than likely the problems will keep arising. If you invest in yourself, your whole world will change for the better. The most important thing to remember is you are worthy; you deserve to put effort into yourself and show yourself self-love. You are perfect because you are you and that is the very reason you are here.

Finding our Paradise

One of the last words David spoke before his accident as he looked out onto the lake was that, 'this place is paradise'. I believe now that was his soul referring to the place he was going to next and this gives me so much comfort. I imagine David as that little water beetle from the poem turning into the most magnificent dragonfly, with wings so blue they sparkle in the sun.

I now have an understanding and acceptance that it was David's time to leave this physical world, just like one day it will be mine and one day it will be yours. David had completed what he was supposed to do here in this lifetime and, just like that, he was called back home. A home that is so beautiful that he referred to it as 'paradise'.

As ironic as it sounds, I feel like on this journey I found my inner paradise. I did not ever imagine I could find my wings and in finding them, I would soar so high. David was the water beetle that transformed into the beautiful dragonfly. I was a caterpillar that transformed into a beautiful butterfly. I had to shed all my old layers. The layers of grief that I held on to so tightly because they were all I knew. As I started to shed the layers and learn to love myself, I began to let the light in and then I began to flourish. With each glimmer of light and a good nudge from David, I began to navigate and find joy in this new life. A life of meaning that finds joyful bliss in all the small things in life such as wrapping your hands around a warm cup of coffee in the morning and having loving connections with friends and family.

I began to fully understand the realisation that this world around us can be a beautiful place if we just believe. I say 'we' because the most important thing I learnt is that everything in life comes back to us. We can choose in any given moment how we react to the challenges in our lives.

We get to decide how we view the world around us. To guide us, we have the most beautiful tool. Our heart. When we act and serve others from our heart space, we can do no wrong. Magic surrounds us daily. Open your eyes and don't be surprised at what you may find.

The Dragonfly and the Butterfly Watch the Beautiful Night Sky Together

One night recently, I remember looking out at the most beautiful, majestic red sky. My soul felt so drawn to it, I felt so inspired and uplifted, and it sparked an inner joy within me. I stared at that sky and gratitude invoked all my senses—appreciation for the sky and my ability to see it. I could feel the joyful energy lifting up my body and I, too was grateful for this.

I knew I was fully conscious and present, looking up at that beautiful sky. My mind was nowhere else, energy rushing through my body.

In that moment, I too, was in paradise. Tears started to roll down my cheeks. These were not sad tears; these were happy tears. Tears of courage, of growth but mostly filled with so much love. I stared at that sky like I had never stared at a sky before. I imagined David's soul looking out onto his paradise at the lake just before his accident.

A memory that once brought me so much heartache, now an image that began to soothe my soul. I thanked David for sending me on this journey. He helped me heal, grow and transform into a butterfly to enable me to spread my wings.

I thanked him for taking away everything from me to complete me and make me feel whole again. I had a natter with him as if he were standing right beside me. I felt his presence so strong, his essence, his soul. I knew he was there. I felt embraced by his energy. In that moment, I did not need anything. I was in bliss knowing everything was perfect.

I started to laugh at the comic my life had become in the most fantastic way possible. In that moment I felt so full of love because I knew it was not just me staring out at that beautiful red sky, David was there too. The dragonfly and the butterfly watching the night sky, full of pride, love, and admiration for each other. On this journey, their souls would remain intertwined.

When David left, our love story continued and he showed me that, no matter what, love always prevails. He was gone in the physical sense, but he was going to guide me and make sure I would create the life I deserved - even if it meant without him.

Where to Find the Author

Email: ciaraomwellness@gmail.com

Instagram: Ciara O'Malley- ciaraomwellness

Facebook: Ciara O'Malley- ciaraomwellness

Twitter: Ciara O'Malley